Native Trees

of Western Washington

Native Trees

of Western Washington

A PHOTOGRAPHIC GUIDE

KEVIN W. ZOBRIST

WSU PRESS

Washington State University
Pullman, Washington

WASHINGTON STATE
UNIVERSITY

Washington State University Press
PO Box 645910
Pullman, Washington 99164-5910
Phone: 800-354-7360
Fax: 509-335-8568
Email: wsupress@wsu.edu
Website: wsupress.wsu.edu

Scripture taken from the Holy Bible, NEW INTERNATIONAL VERSION®. Copyright © 1973, 1978, 1984 by Biblica, Inc. All rights reserved worldwide. Used by permission.

Library of Congress Cataloging-in-Publication Data

Zobrist, Kevin
 Native trees of western Washington : a photographic guide / Kevin W. Zobrist.
    pages cm
 Includes bibliographical references and index.
 ISBN 978-0-87422-324-8 (alk. paper)
 1. Trees—Washington (State). 2. Endemic plants—Washington (State).
 I. Title.
 QK192.Z63 2014
 582.1609797'6—dc23

                                                                        2014019565

This book is dedicated to my mom—
always my best editor
and writing coach.

You will go out in joy and be led forth in peace;

the mountains and hills will burst into song before you,

and all the trees of the field will clap their hands.

Isaiah 55:12

Table of Contents

Acknowledgments

I owe thanks to a number of people for helping make this project possible. I thank all of my forestry colleagues from WSU Extension, the Washington Department of Natural Resources, and the King County Department of Natural Resources and Parks, especially Don Hanley and John Keller, for their support and for helping me learn in the days when I couldn't tell fir trees apart. Thanks to Mary Ann Rozance for the GIS work with the tree range maps. Thanks also to all of the manuscript reviewers—their sound advice greatly improved this book. Finally, many thanks to my wife Lisa for her encouragement, support, and patience throughout this project.

Parts of this book are adapted from three online learning modules produced by WSU Extension: "Native Trees of Western Washington" (Zobrist 2011), "More Native Trees of Western Washington" (Zobrist 2011), and "Forest Stand Dynamics in Western Washington" (Zobrist 2012). These modules are available from WSU Extension at forestry.wsu.edu.

Introduction

Forests are the dominant land cover in western Washington and are among the state's most important natural assets. Residents and visitors alike value them for the beauty, recreation opportunities, and habitat they provide. As an Extension forestry specialist for Washington State University, I am frequently asked not only about tree identification, but also about what makes a particular species unique. This is not a botany book and not intended as a field guide or identification key—there are several excellent books of this type already available (see references). Rather, this book looks at native trees from a forestry perspective, providing a photographic guide that illustrates the key features of native trees found growing in western Washington, information on where to find them, and brief discussions of each tree's notable features.

This book also briefly lists some common human uses of many of the species, based on a variety of sources (see references). Uses are divided into two types. "Traditional" refers to Native American uses for medicinals, food, materials, etc. "Modern" refers to commercial uses from the time of European settlement up to present day. These categorizations are not meant to imply that traditional uses are no longer in practice today nor that all the modern uses are still in practice. An emphasis is placed on uses employed specifically in western Washington. Some species do not have uses specified because their rarity in western Washington results in a lack of information about traditional uses and a lack of marketable quantities for modern uses in this specific part of the region. There may be different traditional and modern uses in other parts of the Northwest for the same species. These lists are not exhaustive—there are excellent books available that describe human uses in greater detail (see references).

Information was gathered from a number of sources, as well as my own experience and observations. A reference list of sources used is provided at the end of the text. I highly recommend each listed reference for further reading and study. If you have an interest in native trees and plants in western Washington, you will find any of these to be welcome additions to your bookshelf.

This book is organized into five sections. This introductory section explains basic tree physiology and forest stand dynamics, a key part of forest ecology. The next section covers common lowland conifers, followed by common lowland broad-leaved trees. The fourth section focuses on the high-elevation species found in the Olympic Mountains and the western side of the Cascade Mountains. The final section covers species that have a very limited natural range in western Washington, with only small, isolated populations (these trees may be common in other parts of the region, though).

Following these five sections are detailed lists of species organized by various categories. A glossary follows, offering definitions of scientific and technical terms utilized throughout the book.

What is a tree?

In most cases the consideration of whether or not a species qualifies as a tree is straightforward. However, several species could be considered either a small tree or a large woody shrub. There are also species generally found as shrubs that occasionally form a tree, as well as species generally found as trees that occasionally form shrub thickets, depending on the growing conditions.

Ultimately, classification of these borderline species is somewhat arbitrary and not terribly critical. The working definition of a tree used for this book is a species that is usually single-stemmed for at least the first few feet above the ground and reaches heights of greater than 30 feet (9 m) at maturity. Under this definition, several species that are often considered trees have been excluded, such as vine maple, beaked hazelnut, black hawthorn, serviceberry, and some of the willows. Numerous available plant guides cover these large woody shrub species.

Coniferous vs. broad-leaved trees

Trees are divided between two key types: conifer and broad-leaved. Conifers are also commonly referred to as evergreens or softwoods, while broad-leaved trees are referred to as deciduous or hardwoods. These common terms are not always accurate, as some conifers are not evergreen (e.g., the larches that grow in eastern Washington), and some evergreen trees like the madrone are broad-leaved. Even the term conifer can sometimes seem like a misnomer, such as with yews or junipers, whose modified cone structures are more berry-like. Perhaps the most technically accurate terms are gymnosperms (which means naked seeds, referring to the seeds not being enclosed in an ovary) for the conifers, and angiosperms (seeds enclosed in an ovary) for the broad-leaved trees. You will often encounter these various terms used interchangeably.

Basic tree physiology

To understand trees, it helps to know a little bit about their physiology. Photosynthesis is their fundamental process. Forests are solar-powered systems, and sunlight supplies the energy that flows through these systems. How trees grow and respond to conditions all relates back to this process. Photosynthesis is the process by which trees and other plants take in carbon dioxide and water and convert the molecules to oxygen, which is released back into the air, and sugars, which are used or stored as food to provide for life functions and growth. This rearrangement of molecules requires energy. Photosynthesis uses light energy from the sun, which becomes chemical energy that is stored within the molecular bonds of the sugars and subsequently the tissues of the tree.

Through photosynthesis, carbon that had previously been in the form of carbon dioxide in the atmosphere becomes part of the sugar molecules and the subsequent tissues of the tree. This is what is referred to as carbon sequestration—trees remove carbon dioxide from the atmosphere and store the carbon in solid form, primarily in their woody stems. If the tree tissues remain intact, the carbon remains sequestered. Thus logs and lumber continue to store carbon and keep it out of the atmosphere. If the tree tissues (e.g., wood) burn or decompose, the molecular bonds break, releasing the stored energy in the form of heat, and the carbon is released back into the atmosphere in the form of carbon dioxide. This is part of what is known as the carbon cycle.

Trees have three key parts: the crown, the stem, and the roots. The crown (i.e., the foliage) is where photosynthesis occurs. The leaves serve as natural solar collectors, and they also take in carbon dioxide from the air through tiny pores called stomata. The roots draw in water from the soil through osmosis, along with dissolved chemicals like nitrogen, phosphorous, and potassium (referred to henceforth as nutrients) necessary for survival and growth. The stem's job is to transport resources between the crown and the roots. Sugars produced in the leaves by photosynthesis are transported down the stem to feed and maintain the roots and other parts of the tree. Water and dissolved nutrients are transported up the stem from the roots to the crown to be used in the photosynthesis process.

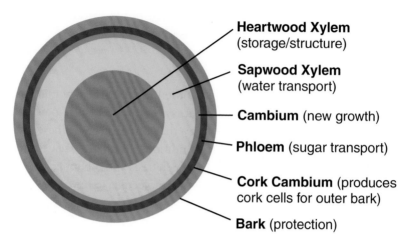

Heartwood Xylem (storage/structure)

Sapwood Xylem (water transport)

Cambium (new growth)

Phloem (sugar transport)

Cork Cambium (produces cork cells for outer bark)

Bark (protection)

Figure 1: Cross-section of a tree stem.

The upward transport of water (with dissolved nutrients) is thought to take place primarily through transpiration pull. When the stomata on the leaves open to allow outside air (containing carbon dioxide) to flow in, oxygen and water vapor escape. This outflow of water vapor, known as transpiration, creates negative pressure that draws replacement water from the surrounding tissue. By the molecular forces of cohesion and adhesion, this pulls a continuous column of water all the way up through the tree's vascular system from the roots to the leaves to replace the water that was lost. The tree cells are passive in this process, acting as tiny pipe-like vessels rather than supplying any force or energy.

The tree stem comprises specific layers (figure 1), and each of these layers has different functions. The majority of the stem is composed of xylem, or what we might simply call "wood." There are two types of xylem: sapwood and heartwood. When the tree is young, all of the xylem is sapwood. Sapwood functions as the tree's plumbing system, with cells forming tiny pipelines that carry water with dissolved nutrients to the top of the tree. As the tree grows in diameter, there is more sapwood than needed for water transport. The oldest (innermost) xylem morphs into heartwood. To become heartwood, the xylem cells die and resins and other chemicals are deposited there, making it darker in color and more resistant to decay. Heartwood is dead and does not transport water, but functions as structural support.

Around the outside of the sapwood is a very thin layer called the vascular cambium. This is where active cell division occurs to produce new layers of xylem on the inside and phloem on the outside. The new xylem added each year will have a light and a dark portion, referred to as the annual rings. In the spring, growth is rapid and the cells are not packed as densely. This growth is called early or spring wood, and it is the light-colored annual ring. As the year progresses, growth slows and the cells are packed more tightly with thicker cell walls forming the denser, dark-colored ring called late or summer wood. Thus a pair of light and dark rings represents one year's growth.

Immediately outside the cambium is the phloem or inner bark. This living tissue is responsible for taking the sugars produced by the leaves and transporting them down to the roots and other parts of the tree. Girdling, or cutting through the phloem layer all the way around a tree, causes the tree to die by cutting off the sugar transport and starving the roots.

The outermost layer of the stem is the outer bark, which serves to protect the tree. The outer bark is composed of cork cells, produced by another thin cambium layer, the cork cambium, located directly under the outer bark outside the phloem.

Why trees grow where they do

All trees need three key resources to survive and grow: sunlight, water, and nutrients. They also need carbon dioxide, but this is not likely to be a limiting factor. While all species share these same basic needs, different species have specific biological adaptations to different types of conditions. These adaptations may allow a species to tolerate things such as shade, wet soils, extreme temperatures, or snow loads. These adaptations are part of a tree's silvical characteristics (growth traits) that govern why different tree species tend to be found at different places on the landscape and at different life stages of the forest.

A tree's tolerance is not necessarily its preference. For instance, some shade-tolerant species may actually prefer (grow better in) full sunlight, but can survive in the shade where other species might not. Thus, where a species grows in both space and time is not necessarily based on its ideal habitat, but sometimes is a matter of competitive advantage, or where it can use its particular adaptations to outcompete other species under given circumstances.

What does it mean to be native?

Native species are those that naturally occur in an area as opposed to having been introduced by humans. Where a tree grows natively is known as its range or distribution. Native trees are suitably adapted to the growing conditions (e.g., climate and soils) within their range such that they successfully perpetuate and thrive.

Non-native species have been introduced from other areas, and are often planted in gardens and landscaping for aesthetic purposes. These are referred to as ornamental species. Trees that are cultivated for fruit or nut production (i.e., orchard trees) are usually non-native. Non-native species can grow and reproduce successfully when planted and tended, though they may be prone to some problems (especially weather-related) as a result of being outside their natural range. In forested areas, though, they will not usually compete successfully with better-adapted native flora.

Some non-native species adapt well to a new location and do successfully compete with native flora and spread widely. These are known as invasive species. These species would not have occurred naturally in their new location due to natural migration barriers (e.g., their natural range is on a different continent). Humans provide artificial vectors for importation of these species, either purposely (e.g., as ornamentals) or accidentally. Once established, these species may unexpectedly spread rapidly and begin to out-compete the native vegetation. Invasive species can be particularly aggressive due to the absence of the natural controls (e.g., insects, diseases) with which they have coevolved in their native range.

This book deals only with trees native to western Washington, defined here as the part of the state west of the Cascade Crest. There are other trees that you will encounter throughout western Washington that are not included in this book because they are ornamental, invasive, an agricultural cultivar, or a hybrid between two species. Also, being native is site-specific. For example, a tree may be native to western Washington, but only at high elevations. If found at low elevations it was planted as an ornamental.

Identifying a species

Trees can be identified by several different features: leaves, buds, branching patterns, cones, bark, size and shape, or even smell. Sometimes a tree species will have a single, distinctive feature that is sufficient to provide a conclusive identification. More often, though, examining a combination of features is necessary to accurately identify a species. Examining the growing conditions (e.g., wet vs. dry, high elevation vs. low elevation, etc.) can also be helpful in tree identification.

One of the challenges in species identification is that there can be wide variability in appearance (i.e., different phenotypes) within a given species, depending on factors like age, location, growing conditions, and underlying genetic variability. Tree bark is particularly variable (for example, see the bark images in the Douglas-fir chapter) and is often insufficient to correctly identify a species. Becoming proficient in field identification takes practice.

The cycle of forest development

Understanding the basic life cycle of western Washington forests aids tree identification, as different trees dominate at different life stages. Recognizing the life stage of a forest can provide clues to what species are most likely present. Several models of forest growth and development have been espoused by ecologists and silviculturists. The model presented here is based on Oliver and Larson (see references), because its relative simplicity lends itself well to illustrating key concepts.

A "stand" is a group of trees growing together. Multiple trees form a stand, and multiple stands make up the landscape. Stands are characterized by contiguous areas of similarity in species mix, age, and conditions. For instance, an area of predominantly mature Douglas-fir would be considered a separate stand from an area of young Douglas-fir seedlings or an area dominated by red alder. Soils, topography, and management or disturbance history are some of the factors that give rise to different stands.

A forest development cycle both begins and ends with a stand-replacing disturbance—an event that kills the majority of the trees in the stand, creating open space where a new stand can begin growing. Forest fires, catastrophic windstorms, floods, landslides, volcanic eruptions, and clear-cut logging are some examples of stand-replacing disturbances in western Washington.

After a stand-replacing disturbance, the first stage of forest development, called stand initiation, begins. Plentiful sunlight and moisture and a lack of competition from other trees characterize this stage, allowing many new trees and plants to begin growing (figure 2). The process of a

Figure 2: Stand initiation is characterized by plentiful growing resources that allow many new trees and plants to begin growing.

stand-replacing disturbance followed by re-colonization with new trees results in what we call an even-aged stand. The trees in the new stand all start growing at approximately the same time and are all approximately the same age. Stands will remain even-aged in nature until later stages of development.

As the new trees get bigger and start to spread their crowns, the canopy closes, cutting off light to the forest floor. This dark, dense second stage is called stem exclusion, because conditions no longer favor the establishment of new trees (figure 3). During the stem-exclusion stage, the forest floor vegetation may be very sparse or die off completely because of lack of sunlight.

As competition for resources continues, some trees, for instance a slightly taller tree with more access to sunlight, will out-compete others. Those unable to successfully compete become subject to overtopping and thus further loss of resources. Some of these trees will die as a result. When individual and groups of trees die, it opens up areas of increased sunlight, promoting new understory vegetation growth, including shrubs and tree seedlings. This stage, called understory reinitiation (figure 4), happens

Figure 3: Stem exclusion is characterized by dark, dense conditions.

Figure 4: In understory reinitiation, areas of increased sunlight open up to allow new understory vegetation growth.

Figure 5: Old growth is characterized by highly diverse and complex structure.

sporadically over many years. Trees that establish under an existing canopy are called advanced regeneration.

In the absence of other disturbances, overstory trees will continue to die off as individuals or in small groups, and understory trees will rise up to take their place. Dead wood will accumulate, including standing dead trees, called snags, and downed logs, which are also referred to as coarse woody debris. If these processes proceed for several centuries without another major disturbance, the result is the old-growth stage, which is characterized by highly diverse and complex structure (figure 5). Multiple canopy layers and age diversity will develop as advanced regeneration is established and gaps are filled with new trees.

Lowland Conifers

1. Douglas-fir

(*Pseudotsuga menziesii*)
Pine family (*Pinaceae*)

Douglas-fir is perhaps the quintes-
sential western Washington tree, and
it dominates lowland forests. Its fast
growth and superior wood strength
make it commercially desirable and
the region's most important lumber
species. Douglas-fir is a versatile tree found
throughout western North America, with different forms and characteristics depending on the environment. The larger coastal form, subspecies
menziesii, grows in western Washington.

Douglas-fir is not one of the true firs
(which are in the *Abies* genus), and its name
is hyphenated to reflect that. Douglas-fir was
confusing to early botanists, who referred to it
as a pine, spruce, true fir, and hemlock before
categorizing it separately as Douglas-fir. There
is only one other type of Douglas-fir in North
America, which is a small tree in southern
California called the bigcone Douglas-fir. The
scientific genus name *Pseudotsuga* actually
means "false hemlock." The common and scientific names both give credit to Scottish botanists who studied it, Archibald Menzies and
David Douglas.

Bark of mature Douglas-fir.

Douglas-fir is found throughout western
Washington. It is in the pine family, which comprises trees with needles. It is the largest mem-
ber of this family, growing tall and straight with
a pyramidal top. It has several distinguishing
characteristics that make it easy to identify. On
mature trees, it develops characteristic deeply-furrowed brown bark, though on younger
trees the bark can be smooth, blistered, and

One form of immature
Douglas-fir bark.

sometimes light-colored. The Douglas-fir has light green needles with two white bands on the underside. These are referred to as stomatal bands, as this is where the stomata, or breathing pores, are located. Douglas-fir has needles arranged spirally around the twig like a bottlebrush,

and the brown, lanceolate (like the tips of spears) buds are distinctive of this species. The needles smell like citrus if you crush them.

Douglas-fir seed cones are pendant cones, hanging down from the branch like a necklace pendant. They are three to four inches long at maturity, with three-pronged woody bracts sticking out. Folklore concerning these bracts describes a great fire or storm in the forest in which the mice take refuge in the Douglas-fir cones, with just their tails and back legs sticking out. No other tree has a cone like this, so when you see those little mouse tails, you know it is a Douglas-fir. In the spring the tree also has many small reddish-brown pollen cones.

One of the most important things to know about Douglas-fir is that it is shade intolerant, a key silvical characteristic, especially the coastal subspecies that occurs in western Washington. The subspecies found east of the Cascades is a little more shade tolerant. Coastal Douglas-fir needs open areas with full sunlight and exposed soil, such as after a major disturbance like fire or logging, for successful regeneration.

Douglas-fir has a fast juvenile growth rate of 20–30 feet (6–9 m) in the first ten years on a good site with abundant sunlight. It will not tolerate wet, saturated soils or extreme cold, thus preferring lower elevations but not swampy areas. It has some limited drought tolerance. Mature Douglas-fir is well-adapted to fire. Its thick bark insulates and protects it from lower-intensity fires which remove competing vegetation. For large, catastrophic fires hot enough to kill mature Douglas-fir, its regeneration abilities in open areas, along with its fast early growth, give it an advantage to re-colonize a fire-ravaged site. Many of the pre-settlement old-growth Douglas-fir stands of the western Cascades were likely originated by large, catastrophic fires.

Douglas-fir can live up to 750 years or more and reach heights of 200–300 feet (60–90 m) and diameters of 10–15 feet (3–4.5 m). It is fairly well-rooted, forming a taproot in its early years (depending on the soil depth) and grafting with roots of surrounding trees as it ages and its root system expands. It is highly susceptible to several fungal root diseases. The root grafting with other individuals can spread root disease from tree to tree, creating a circular pattern of mortality and decline known as a root disease or root rot pocket. Live infected trees may topple when too much of the root system or lower stem rots away, or they may first die standing and then eventually topple. Unlike eastern Washington, where bark beetle infestations are a major forest health concern, root rot tends to be the dominant forest health issue in western Washington coniferous forests.

Quick facts about Douglas-fir:

- Shade intolerant
- Fast growth rate
- Intolerant of wet soils
- Fire-resistant bark
- Life span of 750+ years
- Reaches heights of 200–300 feet
- Susceptible to root diseases

Common uses:

Traditional
- Wood: firewood and various tools and implements
- Pitchy wood: torches
- Pitch: sealant, salves, chewing gum
- Needles: boiled to make a tea

Modern
- Wood: dimensional lumber, plywood, and other wood products
- Christmas trees

2. Western hemlock

(*Tsuga heterophylla*)
Pine family (*Pinaceae*)

Western hemlock, found throughout western Washington and a close associate of Douglas-fir, is the state tree of Washington. Commercial uses include lumber, plywood, and paper products. Western hemlock can be identified from a distance based on its silhouette with a characteristic droopy top. Western hemlock has no relation to the poison hemlock that killed Socrates, but supposedly the crushed leaves have a similar smell, which is how it got its common name.

The short and blunt-tipped needles form flat sprays, green on top with two white stomatal bands on the bottom. The mix of longer and shorter needles is reflected in the scientific name *Tsuga heterophylla*, with *heterophylla* meaning different leaves. *Tsuga* is derived

from the Japanese word meaning mother tree. The bark is rough, but not nearly as thick or deeply furrowed as Douglas-fir. Western hemlock seed cones are small egg-shaped pendants approximately 1 inch (2.5 cm) long.

The needles are short and blunt-tipped, forming flat sprays.

Western hemlock is very shade tolerant, and often found growing in the understory. When grown in the open it has a moderate juvenile growth rate of approximately 15 feet (4.5 m) in the first

Shade tolerance allows western hemlock to grow in the understory.

ten years on a good site. It prefers moist, but not wet areas, and it will not tolerate continually wet or droughty soils. It typically grows up to 200 feet (60 m) tall and 4 feet (1.2 m) in diameter (though it can grow larger), with a life span usually in the neighborhood of 200–400 years—shorter than some of its associates. Western hemlock is not a very resilient species. It has thin bark and shallow roots (it does not form a taproot), making it very susceptible to mechanical injury, windthrow, soil disturbance, and disease.

Although subject to many mortality agents, western hemlock's regeneration abilities and high tolerance of shade help the species' success. It prolifically seeds, sometimes creating a dense carpet of seedlings on the forest floor. Because of its shade tolerance, it can survive in this shaded understory environment until an overstory gap opens up. Because of this ability to perpetuate itself even under its own shade, western hemlock can begin to dominate lowland forests in the long-term absence of disturbance.

Quick facts about western hemlock:

- Very shade tolerant
- Moderate growth rate
- Likes moist but not wet areas
- Lives 200–400 years
- Reaches heights of 200 feet
- Thin bark and shallow roots
- Prolific regeneration
- State tree of Washington

Common uses:

Traditional
- Wood: firewood and various tools and implements
- Bark: tanning solutions and various dyes
- Boughs: bedding material, implements for collecting herring spawn
- Pitch: salves, poultices, liniments, chest rub (for colds), sunscreen

Modern
- Wood: dimensional lumber, plywood, pilings, poles, railroad ties, flooring
- Pulp: paper, rayon fabric

3. Western redcedar

(*Thuja plicata*)
Cypress family (*Cupressaceae*)

Western redcedar, one of the hardiest and longest-lived Northwest
trees, is very important to Native
Americans, and is commercially
prized for its fragrant, decay-resistant wood used for many applications.
Western redcedar generally has the highest value
per board foot of the main commercial lumber trees
in western Washington.

Found throughout western Washington, western redcedar's unique
foliage gives it a distinctive look. Fragrant and luxuriant, it hangs from
the branches and is composed of overlapping scales rather than needles.
White waxy patches on the undersides of the leaves can look like little
x's or butterflies. Western redcedar produces clusters of cones that are
round and very small, approximately 0.5 inch (1.3 cm) long. The cones

look like little woody flowers when
they open. The reddish-brown bark
is thin and stringy, and the base of
older redcedar trees may become
swollen and fluted with wavy
ridges. The aromatic foliage, with
its sweet and fruity fragrance, is
highly preferred by deer and elk for
food. When trying to grow western
redcedar, seedling tops may need
protection until they are above the
height of browsing animals.

Western redcedar is not a true
cedar. True cedars have needles and
are thus in the pine family. They
are not native to North America,
but rather to the Himalayan and
Mediterranean regions. Redcedar

is written as one word, to distinguish it as one of our "false cedars," which are actually in the cypress family. Cedar refers to fragrant wood, which is how western redcedar got its common name. Western redcedar is in the *Thuja* genus, making it an arborvitae, meaning tree of life, and giant arborvitae is another common name for western redcedar. *Thuja* also means fragrant wood, and *plicata* means folded leaves.

Western redcedar has a moderate juvenile grow rate of approximately 15 feet (4.5 m) in the first ten years when grown on an open, good site. It

prefers moist sites and is not tolerant of drought, but is tolerant of wet soils, and is often the conifer you will find growing in wet areas, though it will not survive extended inundation.

Western redcedar is resistant to the root diseases that frequently affect other conifers. It does not form a taproot, but has a dense, abundant root network deeper than western hemlock but shallower than Douglas-fir. Despite its general resistance to decay, it is vulnerable to stem diseases like butt rot. This rotten wood may in turn be subject to carpenter ants, and you will sometimes see large rectangular cavities excavated out of the trunk by a pileated woodpecker feeding on these ants. Western redcedar is also vulnerable to storm damage, with older trees often losing tops multiple times, resulting in a multi-forked top that resembles a candelabra. What sets western redcedar apart from other species is its resilience in the face of physical injury and stem decay. You may encounter a redcedar with the inside of the trunk completely rotted away, yet the tree continues to survive and support itself by a thin outer ring of sound wood. These resilient qualities make it one of the region's longest-lived species, sometimes over 1,000 years old. It can grow up to 200 feet (60 m) tall and 20 feet (6 m) in diameter.

Western redcedar was a particularly important tree for Native Americans, who used it extensively. Planks, bark, and roots were usually cut from living trees rather than felling them, which was possible because of the tree's resilience to injury.

Quick facts about western redcedar:

- Shade tolerant
- Medium growth rate
- Tolerates wet sites
- Lives 1,000+ years
- Reaches heights of 200 feet
- Resistant to disease and injury
- Decay-resistant wood

Common uses:

Traditional
- Wood: firewood, houses, dugout canoes, boxes, friction fire-starter sets, and numerous tools and implements
- Bark: clothing, baskets, rope, tinder, sanitary pads, diapers
- Roots: baskets
- Branches: rope
- Leaf tips and buds: various medicinal uses

Modern
- Wood: decking, siding, shingles, shakes, fence posts, clothing chests, paneling, kindling

Cedar flagging

In early fall, the innermost foliage of the western redcedar turns orange or brown, which is called "flagging." This is a normal, seasonal phenomenon and not cause for concern, but rather the process of the tree shedding its oldest foliage. All conifers do this to some degree, but it is most pronounced in western redcedar. The flagging foliage will blow away with the fall and winter winds, and the following spring the tree will produce new foliage at the ends of the branches.

4. Grand fir

(*Abies grandis*)
Pine family (*Pinaceae*)

Grand fir is one of the true firs, which are in the *Abies* genus. It is sometimes referred to as white fir, but this causes confusion as white fir is a separate species (*Abies concolor*) that does not grow north of southern Oregon. True firs

have several traits in common. One is that they have rounded buds, with the terminal bud often being a cluster of three. This results in a more regulated and symmetrical branching pattern compared to Douglas-fir or western hemlock. Another true fir characteristic is the circular "suction cup" leaf attachment to the stem. If you pluck off a leaf, you should notice a distinct circular leaf scar. True fir cones are cylindrical and form at the top of the tree, and they grow upright instead of hanging down. When the cones mature, they will shed layer by layer (often with the help

of hungry squirrels) leaving a bare central stalk in the middle. Grand fir cones are approximately 4 inches (10 cm) long.

Grand fir is the true fir that is most common to the lowlands. Other western Washington true firs grow either mostly or exclusively at higher elevations. Grand fir's range extends throughout western Washington.

The cones shed their layers, leaving a bare central stalk.

It tends to be more prevalent on drier sites such as rain shadow areas (e.g., Whidbey Island, the San Juans, and northeast Olympic Peninsula) where it can better compete with shade-tolerant conifers that are less tolerant of dry conditions. You will also tend to find it in cooler areas such as throughout Whatcom County and in cool drainages in the Cascade foothills. You will typically find it as part of mixed conifer stands, though in Whatcom County it is often found together with paper birch.

Grand fir has flat needles that are a rich glossy green on top with two very pronounced white stomatal bands underneath. These leaves are somewhat similar to Douglas-fir. However, whereas Douglas-fir has needles spirally arranged on all sides of the twig, grand fir needles are two-ranked, meaning that they grow in two distinct rows opposite each other on either side of the twig. Grand fir leaves are very aromatic, with a rich, balsam scent.

Abies means tall or rising, and *grandis* means large.

True to its name, grand fir can be a very well-formed tree reaching heights of over 200 feet (60 m). In windy areas like Whidbey Island, where the tree is common, it often has a flat, sheared-off top or multiple tops as a result of storm damage. The bark is fairly smooth with resin blisters when the tree is younger, but it will become rougher as the tree ages, often with bright yellowish-green lichen patches.

Grand fir is shade tolerant, though not to the degree of western hemlock or western redcedar. Grand fir is more deeply-rooted than western hemlock or western redcedar, but not as deep as Douglas-fir. It generally forms a taproot, especially on dry sites, aiding survival in dry, exposed conditions. It is a thin-barked tree that does not have resinous wood, making it susceptible to injury, disease, and fire. Grand fir can live to be 200–300 years old.

Quick facts about grand fir:

- Typically found on dry or cool low-elevation sites
- Shade tolerant
- Can live 200–300 years
- Reaches heights of 200 feet
- Susceptible to injury, disease, and fire

Common uses:

Traditional

- Wood knots: fish hooks
- Bark: brown dye, boiled as a tonic and for baths
- Boughs: incense, air freshener
- Needles: boiled to make a medicinal tea (for colds)

Modern

- Wood: low-strength lumber
- Pulp: paper
- Christmas trees

5. Sitka spruce
(*Picea sitchensis*)
Pine family (*Pinaceae*)

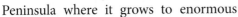

Sitka spruce, an impressive tree that grows in cool, moist areas, can be found throughout the western Washington lowlands, most prevalently in the rain- and fog-soaked coastal areas along the western Olympic Peninsula where it grows to enormous

proportions. Though not as common further inland, it can be found on cool, moist sites or near Puget Sound shorelines. The genus name *Picea* means pitch-producing, and both the common and scientific names refer to Sitka, Alaska. Spruce means "from Prussia."

A mature Sitka spruce is tall with sweeping branches that tend to curve upward. At ground level it can be identified by its bark alone. This distinct bark, which ranges in color from light gray to reddish-brown, has prominent, flaky scales. The sharp, stiff needles are prickly (even painful) to the touch. Like all spruce trees, the needles grow from little woody pegs. In contrast to the sharp needles, the cones of the Sitka spruce are soft pendant cones with thin, papery scales.

Windswept Sitka spruces are common along coastal beaches.

Sitka spruce is shade tolerant, though not as much as western hemlock or western redcedar. As such, disturbed areas help it become established among these common coastal forest cohorts. Sitka spruce tolerates salt spray, and thus is common along coastal beaches in a stunted, windswept form. Living up to 800 years, it is one of the largest conifers in western Washington, attaining heights of 200–300 feet (60–90 m) and diameters up to 10 feet (3 m). Long lateral roots are not particularly deep, though deeper soils will allow downward growth.

Sitka spruce wood is soft, lightweight, and very strong. This high strength-to-weight ratio made it desirable for use in wooden aircraft in the early twentieth century. The wood also has superior acoustic properties, making it desirable for use in musical instruments.

Sitka spruce often becomes deformed by two common insect pests. One is the spruce tip weevil (*Pissodes strobe*), also called the white pine weevil, which kills the leader of the tree. Spruce growing in open, sunny conditions are particularly prone to this pest, which thrives in warm conditions. The other is the Cooley spruce gall adelgid, which causes the branch tips to develop swollen galls that almost resemble cones. The cool, foggy conditions of

Cooley spruce gall adelgid damage.

the coast help keep these insect pests at bay, with the trees being more susceptible further inland.

Quick facts about Sitka spruce:

- Most common on the coast, near Puget Sound shorelines, or inland on cool, moist sites
- Shade tolerant
- Lives up to 800 years
- Reaches heights of 200–300 feet
- Often impacted by the spruce tip weevil or the Cooley spruce gall adelgid, especially away from the coast conditions.

Common uses:

Traditional

- Roots: baskets, rain hats
- Pitch: chewing gum, sealant, salves, medicine for sore throats and other ailments
- Shoots: eaten raw by the Makah

Modern

- Wood: musical instruments, sounding boards, aircraft, dimensional lumber
- Poles: ship masts

6. Western white pine

(*Pinus monticola*)
Pine family (*Pinaceae*)

The stately western white pine is found throughout much of western Washington. Pine trees bear their needles in bundles called fascicles, and white pines are five-needle pines, meaning their long needles come five per bundle. Compared to some other pines, western white pine needles are relatively soft and supple.

A large tree that can grow tall and straight with a slender, symmetrical crown and uniform branch whorls, it has rapid juvenile growth and can reach heights of over 160 feet (50 m). It has platy gray-brown bark and distinctively large, elongated cones that can grow to be ten inches (25 cm) long.

Western white pine has a wide elevation range from sea level to over 5,000 feet (1,525 m). It seems to be particularly common on Whidbey Island, in the San Juans, and along I-5 north of Seattle, as well as in the high-elevation forests of the Cascades and Olympics. Its scientific name, *Pinus monticola*, means pine of the mountains. It tends to grow in mixed conifer stands and prefers moist areas, though it can tolerate poor soils. It has intermediate shade tolerance that makes competition with other more shade-tolerant species difficult in the absence of disturbance. It grows best in open, sunny conditions and can live to be 300 to 400 years old.

White pine blister rust infection.

Western white pine is resistant to some root diseases, making it a possible alternative to Douglas-fir where root disease is a problem. However, it is particularly vulnerable to white pine blister rust, an exotic (Eurasian) fungal disease that has caused large-scale mortality of white pine species across North America since its accidental introduction in 1910.

The blister rust first appears as yellow and red spots on the needles and then forms a canker on the branch, often with orange coloring around the margin. This will eventually girdle and kill the tree once it reaches the stem.

This pine used to be much more prevalent before the introduction of the blister rust, and was a valuable lumber species. There is no treatment for blister rust, but some success breeding trees that have a genetic resistance has been accomplished. The blister rust requires an alternate host to complete its life cycle. Alternate hosts include currants, gooseberries, Indian paintbrush, and lousewort. Planting resistant stock, keeping the trees separated from shrubs like red flowering currant, pruning up lower limbs to improve air circulation, and pruning infected branches before the canker reaches the main stem can increase the chance of western white pine survival. Completely eliminating alternate host species in an area is not effective and merely diminishes shrub species that are important for wildlife.

Quick facts about western white pine:

- Five-needle pine
- Intermediate shade tolerance
- Grows up to 160 feet tall
- Can live 300–400 years
- Wide elevation range

- Tolerant of root rot and poor soils
- Heavily impacted by the exotic white pine blister rust

Common uses:

Traditional
- Bark: baskets, small canoes, medicinal infusions for stomach and other ailments, boiled and applied to cuts
- Pitch: chewed as a gum to treat coughs; sealant

Modern
- Wood: dimensional lumber, window and door frames, molding

7. Lodgepole/ shore pine

(*Pinus contorta*)
Pine family (*Pinaceae*)

Lodgepole pine and shore pine are the same species, but two distinctly different subspecies. The coastal form (subspecies *contorta*, meaning contorted), known as shore pine because of its prevalence on saltwater shores, is a short tree, twisted and gnarled. Lodgepole pine is the mountain form (subspecies *latifolia*, meaning broad-leaved), growing tall and straight. A third variation, called Sierra lodgepole pine (subspecies *murrayana*), can also be found in the southern Washington Cascades and southward. Lodgepole pine got its name from its use as tepee (lodge) poles by Native Americans in the Rocky Mountain and plains regions.

Lodgepole pine is common throughout western North America and is an important lumber species. These trees are found in both mixed and pure stands. In Washington, lodgepole pine is not as common on the west side as on the east of the Cascades. Shore pine, however, is readily found along the coast. Further inland, lodgepole pine is often found in wet areas, such as around the springs and meadows in the Longmire area of Mount Rainier. Both forms are found in the Puget Sound area.

Lodgepole and shore pine have needles in bundles of two, readily distinguishing it from other native pines. The needles are stiff and relatively short. This species has dark, scaly, and thin bark, tending to be darker and

a little thicker on the shore form compared to the lodgepole form. The cones are approximately egg size with sharp prickles on the scales. Shore pine cones open at maturity. Lodgepole pine has serotinous cones that remain closed (glued shut by resin) and can persist on the tree for years. Those cones open and release the seeds when the resin is melted by fire. The lodgepole form is thus dependent on fire for regeneration, both for opening the cones and for creating the open, full-sun conditions required by this very shade-intolerant species. The parent trees are easily killed by fire, though, because of their thin bark.

In western Washington, lodgepole or shore pine has a competitive advantage

The short, twisted shore pine form is common on coastal bluffs.

Lodgepole pine can tolerate swampy areas.

on marginal, nutrient-poor sites. This includes dry, sandy sites such as the coastal bluffs where shore pine is found, and at the opposite end of the spectrum, in wet, swampy areas. It is also very tolerant of frost pockets. These extreme tolerances make this species a good choice for tough sites. On good sites it will usually be out-competed by other species.

Quick facts about lodgepole/shore pine:

- Two distinct forms of the same species
- Very shade intolerant
- Easily killed, but also regenerated, by fire
- Can grow on extreme sites, including dry and sandy sites, wet and swampy sites, and cold frost pockets
- Cones are open on shore pine and closed (serotinous) on lodgepole pine

Common uses:

Traditional
- Pitch (shore): salves, poultices
- Wood (lodgepole): teepee (lodge) poles

Modern
- Wood (lodgepole): firewood, dimensional lumber, fence posts, log homes

8. Pacific yew

(*Taxus brevifolia*)
Yew family (*Taxaceae*)

Pacific yew, also called western yew, is found throughout western Washington, though infrequently. Often it will be a tree that "just doesn't look right," as it may have a gnarled, twisted, or deformed shape. The Pacific yew grows very slowly and usually does not reach heights greater than 50 feet (15 m). It is typically found in the shady understory, and is one of the most shade-tolerant trees. It has a deep and wide root system. The wood is hard, strong, flexible, durable, and decay-resistant. These properties made it desirable for a number of traditional uses.

The foliage is very flat, with short needles that are two-ranked, meaning they are arranged in two rows opposite each other on the twig. The scientific name *brevifolia* means short leaves. New twigs are green, almost the same color as the needles. This can help you quickly identify and distinguish it from other species that may look similar, such as western hemlock. The needles are a lighter green underneath, with two faint stomatal bands, and they come to a distinct point at the end. The

bark is brownish-gray and can be scaly or flaky, revealing smooth areas of pink and purple. An important cancer-fighting drug called paclitaxel (brand name Taxol) can be derived from the bark of the Pacific yew, which led to overharvesting. Interestingly, the drug can also be produced by fungal endophytes associated with Pacific yew. Endophytes are microorganisms that live within but do not harm plants. Paclitaxel is now produced from plantations of various yew species and by full or partial synthesis, relieving the harvest pressure on wild yews.

The yew can reproduce vegetatively, meaning it can sprout from the stump or from cuttings. It also does not produce a typical conifer seed cone, but rather a fleshy red berry-like aril, which is actually a modified cone scale surrounding a large seed. Yew has separate male and female trees (i.e., it is dioecious), with only the females bearing the arils. The arils are known for their toxicity, though some sources indicate that it is only the seed, not the flesh, that is poisonous. Even so, the safest approach is to just leave the arils for the birds and small mammals that utilize them as a food source without problem. Like other yews, the foliage is rumored to be toxic to livestock and domestic animals, though it

serves as an important food source for wildlife species such as moose, elk, and deer.

Quick facts about Pacific yew:

- Widespread but not common
- Typically small and not well-formed
- Very slow growing
- Very shade tolerant
- Usually found in the shaded understory
- New twigs are green
- Poisonous seeds are contained in fleshy arils

Common uses:

Traditional
- Wood: bows, arrows, harpoons, paddles, and various other tools and weapons where a strong but flexible wood was desired

Modern
- Wood: decorative pieces
- Bark: cancer drug

Lowland Broad-leaved Trees

9. Red alder

(*Alnus rubra*)
Birch family (*Betulaceae*)

Red alder is common throughout the
western Washington lowlands. This
species used to be considered a weed
because it competes with Douglas-fir
during regeneration of disturbed sites.
Today, however, alder can be more valuable than
Douglas-fir because of its strong market potential
for furniture, cabinetry, and other specialty uses. Red alder was widely
used by Native Americans for fuel, wooden implements, and medicines,
and it is the preferred wood for smoking salmon.

Red alder is a deciduous tree
with coarsely-toothed leaves that
are green on top and light-colored
with reddish-brown hairs underneath. The edges of the leaves curl
under slightly, which is an identi-
fying characteristic. The leaves are
alternate, meaning that the leaves
will grow out from the left and
right side of the twig in an alter-
nating pattern. It does not have
fall color. Red alder gets its name
from the red dye that can be made
from its inner bark, and from the
red stain that develops over freshly
cut wood. *Alnus* means alder and
rubra means red.

Alder is monoecious, bearing
both male and female flowers on
the same tree. Male flowers are long, cylindrical catkins that first appear in
fall and drop off in the spring. Female flowers also first appear in the fall,
mature into woody strobiles that resemble tiny cones, and remain on the
tree through the following fall. The bark is brownish-gray, thin, smooth,

Male catkins.

Female strobiles.

Patches of white lichen on older bark.

and has horizontal markings called lenticels, which are air-exchange pores similar to the stomata on leaves. The bark of older trees appears lighter with patches of white. These white areas are actually epiphytic lichens. They are crustose lichens, meaning that they form a crust that cannot be separated from the tree bark. They do not harm the tree and are actually an indicator of good air quality, since lichens are very sensitive to pollution.

Red alder is a pioneer species that can quickly colonize disturbed sites. It produces prolific seeds and has a very rapid juvenile growth rate of up to 40 feet (12 m) in the first ten years on a good site. It is very intolerant of shade. Red alder grows in moist areas, and is found in riparian habitats along streams and in bottomlands. While alder arrives and establishes quickly, its glory is short-lived. This species only lives to be about 60 to 80 years old before falling apart and succumbing to rot and breakage. Alder is typically a slender tree, though some larger specimens can grow up to 3 feet (1 m) in diameter and over 120 feet (35 m) tall with a spreading canopy. Young trees that are cut will re-sprout from the stump.

An interesting characteristic of red alder is that it fixes nitrogen. This means it can take nitrogen out of the atmosphere and convert it into a chemical form that can be used by plants. It is not the alder itself that

is doing this, but an acti-
nomycete called Frankia,
which is a filamentous
bacterial endophyte that
grows in symbiosis with
the alder. These bacteria
are found in little orange
nodules on the roots of
the alder. They provide
the alder with nitro-
gen in return for sugars.
The alder's nitrogen-rich
leaves are shed each fall,
decomposing to provide
a natural fertilizer that
enriches the soil.

Orange root nodules contain nitrogen-fixing bacteria.

Quick facts about red alder:

- Very shade intolerant
- Very fast growth rate
- Prolific regeneration on disturbed sites
- Grows in moist areas
- Only lives 60–80 years
- Roots host nitrogen-fixing bacteria

Common uses:

Traditional
- Wood: firewood, paddles, dishes and utensils, salmon smoking, fric-
  tion fire-starter sets
- Bark: dyes, medicinal teas and tonics, food (inner bark)

Modern
- Wood: firewood, furniture, cabinetry

Sitka alder

There is another alder in western Washington called Sitka alder (*Alnus viridis ssp. sinuata*). This is a shrub species that does not reach tree heights. It is common at mid elevations. Sitka alder leaves are different from red alder in that they tend to be darker green and glossier with finely-serrated leaf margins that do not curl under.

Species distribution maps in *Atlas of United States Trees*, by Elbert L. Little Jr., also show small pockets of white alder (*Alnus rhombifolia*) occurrence in western Washington near the west side of Mount Rainier. This author has not been able to find any evidence to verify this, and welcomes input from readers in this regard.

10. Bigleaf maple

(*Acer macrophyllum*)
Maple family (*Aceraceae*)

Bigleaf maple is a common broad-leaved tree found throughout the western Washington lowlands. Its leaves, as the name implies, are large, sometimes more than a foot (30 cm) across, and have five lobes. When looking at bigleaf maple saplings in the spring, when neither the tree nor the leaves have reached their full size, the number of lobes can help you distinguish between it and other, smaller maple species that grow as tall understory shrubs. The scientific name *macrophyllum* means large leaves, while the genus name *Acer* means sharp, referring to the sharply pointed leaf tips that maples have.

Bigleaf maple is an attractive tree in all seasons. In the spring, it puts out hanging clusters of yellow flowers. In

the summer, the rich green leaves create a beautiful canopy. These leaves turn bright yellow and orange in the fall, but not red like many other maples. The flowers, meanwhile, develop

into hard, dry, winged fruits called samaras, each containing a seed. This is an important source of hard mast for wildlife. Often called "helicopter seeds," they twirl and spin on fall breezes like little helicopter rotors. Bigleaf maple has double samaras, growing as joined pairs in a V shape. These may occasionally appear in threes and fours as well.

Even in the winter, when its leaves are gone, the bigleaf maple may still remain adorned with epiphytic mosses and ferns, as the bigleaf maple's moist, calcium-rich bark makes it suitable habitat for epiphytic plants. Epiphytes are organisms that grow on, but do not harm, the host plant. The presence of epiphytic plants on bigleaf maple does not indicate that the tree is in poor health.

Bigleaf maple grows vigorously with a juvenile growth rate of up to 40 feet (12 m) in ten years on a good site. It also sprouts (coppices) prolifically from cut stumps. The tree can be successfully regenerated this way, so long as the many sprouts are thinned early to only two or three dominant stems. The prolific coppicing of bigleaf maple may provide some unwanted competition to Douglas-fir in a recent clear-cut. Unlike red alder, its fast-growing associate, bigleaf maple is shade tolerant. It can live to be over 200 years old and reach 80 feet (25 m) tall, but older trees often succumb to heart rot. When grown in an open setting, the bigleaf maple will have a broad, spreading canopy. When crowded in a forest setting it may be a tall, slender tree.

Bigleaf maple is a versatile tree that can grow on a variety of sites, both wet and dry. It prefers moist but well-drained soil, and is often found in bottomland areas. Its abundant leaf litter can help enrich the soil with organic matter, which is especially important on poorer sites. Its broad, shallow root system allows it to tolerate shallow soils.

The wood is softer than that of other maples, and is not typically used for commercial lumber production. It is used, however, for a variety of specialty products such as furniture, cabinets, veneers, and musical instruments. Maples can develop the highly-prized figured grain pattern, as well as burls that can be used as decorative pieces (burls are abnormal wood growths on the side of the tree, analogous to a tumor). Bigleaf maple is good for firewood, and it can even be tapped to make maple syrup (see sidebar).

Quick facts about bigleaf maple:

- Shade tolerant
- Very fast juvenile growth rate
- Large leaves with five lobes
- Can grow on a variety of sites
- Can live to be over 200 years old
- Bark hosts epiphytic plants

Common uses:

Traditional
- Wood: paddles, cradles, bowls, other domestic implements, sweat lodge frames, wood carving, salmon smoking
- Bark: rope
- Leaves: temporary containers, baking pit covers
- Seed sprouts: food

Modern
- Wood: firewood, furniture, cabinetry, veneer, musical instruments
- Sap: maple syrup
- Burls: decorative pieces

Maple syrup

Syrup has not been produced from bigleaf maple on a major commercial scale, but there is growing interest and some commercial operations are beginning to be established in western Washington. Bigleaf maple does not have a sugar content as high as the sugar maples that grow in the Northeast and thus requires a higher volume of sap to make syrup. Western Washington forests have also not been managed for maple production like the forests of the Northeast. Rather, foresters have usually tried to get rid of maple so it won't compete with Douglas-fir. With intentional management and the right soil conditions, though, maple syrup production could be a viable enterprise. It is a myth that bigleaf maple syrup is not as palatable as that from the Northeast. On the contrary, it produces an exceptional syrup that has rich maple flavor with hints of vanilla and can hold its own against anything the Northeast has to offer. Maple sap is turned into syrup by boiling off the water until the sugar concentration increases from 2–2.5% to approximately 66%. The sap can also be boiled off to only 10% sugar (roughly the concentration in commercial soft drinks) and carbonated to produce an excellent cream soda.

Other maples

Vine maple leaves.

There are two other native maples in western Washington. These are large understory shrubs or occasionally small trees. Vine maple (*Acer circinatum*) is very common throughout western Washington forests, forming arching clumps in the understory. Vine maple leaves have seven to nine lobes. Less common but still found throughout western Washington is the Rocky Mountain or Douglas maple (*Acer glabrum*). Rocky Mountain maple is easy to distinguish from vine maple because its leaves have only three lobes. The range of Rocky Mountain maple extends to eastern Washington, whereas vine maple is only found west of the Cascades. The leaves of both of these species turn bright red in the fall.

Rocky Mountain maple leaves.

11. Black cottonwood

(*Populus trichocarpa*)
Willow family (*Salicaceae*)

Black cottonwood seeds float through the air in cottony tufts in late May and early June, giving the peculiar appearance of snow on warm afternoons. Found throughout western Washington, cottonwood trees grow tall and straight, and they can become quite large. They are the largest broad-leaved trees in the Northwest, growing up to 200 feet (60 m) tall.

The bark of a mature cottonwood tree is hard with deep, pronounced grooves. The leaves are deltoid shaped and resemble the ace of spades, though sometimes on young cottonwood sprouts the leaves may appear long and narrow

like a willow. The thick leaves are dark green on top and pale underneath, offering a shimmering effect when they flutter in the breeze. The leaves often display brown fungal spots. In the fall, the leaves turn a bright golden yellow. Cottonwood trees can have a pronounced scent, especially when the sticky resinous buds open up in the spring, filling the air with a heavy, sweet smell.

Resinous bud.

Black cottonwood bears male and female flowers on separate trees. The female flowers mature into round capsules that open up to release black seeds and the namesake cottony tufts. The scientific name *Populus trichocarpa* means a poplar tree with hairy fruits.

Seed pods.

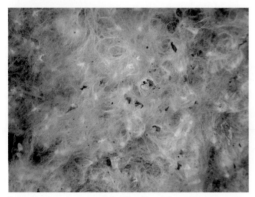
Layers of cottonwood fluff collected on the ground.

Black cottonwood is a pioneer species that colonizes disturbed sites. It prefers moist environments and can tolerate wet areas but not extended inundation. It is not found in hot, dry areas. Cottonwood stems can carry a large volume of water. Cottonwoods are very common in riparian areas along rivers and streams, and especially on floodplains where shifting river channels cause frequent disturbance.

Black cottonwood is very intolerant of shade and has the fastest juvenile growth rate of any native tree in western Washington—over 50 feet (15 m) in ten years. In addition to propagation from its prolific cottony seeds, it can sprout from cut stumps or even branch cuttings. It can live up to 200 years. Where soil conditions allow, it forms a deep and wide root system.

Despite its impressive growth, size, and tough exterior bark, it is a rather weak tree. The wood is soft and rot-prone, and it is notorious for dropping large limbs. Beware of potential hazards around large cottonwoods. Because of its soft wood, black cottonwood lumber tends to be low quality and used for low-strength applications like pallets. Its soft fibers are prized for pulp and paper use, though. Native Americans used black cottonwood for a number of medicinal applications.

Quick facts about black cottonwood:

- Very shade intolerant
- Very fast juvenile growth rate
- Produces cottony seeds
- Grows tall and straight
- Grows in moist to wet areas
- Weak wood

Common uses:

Traditional

- Leaves: bruised to produce an antiseptic for cuts
- Bud resin: salves, poultices, other medicinals, waterproofing
- Burl resin: antiseptic for cuts
- Bark: medicinal infusion, buckets
- Young shoots: sweat lodge frames
- Wood: friction fire-starter sets

Modern

- Wood: low-strength lumber (e.g., pallets)
- Pulp: high-quality paper

12. Bitter cherry

(Prunus emarginata)
Rose family *(Rosaceae)*

Bitter cherry is found throughout western Washington, though
not as commonly as alder, maple,
or cottonwood. It is a shade-intolerant, early-successional species that
quickly establishes following a disturbance and is frequently found in young
forests. Its role is short-lived, though, as it usually
does not remain longer than 50 years. It is not a commercial species.

Bitter cherry can be easy to miss in the forest, where it occurs sporadically with a tall, slender form that tends to blend in. The exception is
in spring, usually around mid-April, when it yields a beautiful display of
abundant white blossoms, making it suddenly one of the most noticeable
trees in the forest. These clusters of white blossoms mature into bright red
fruits. As the name implies, this

Extrafloral nectaries.

fruit is not edible for humans, though it is
enjoyed by wildlife.

Bitter cherry has oval leaves with
finely serrated margins and two tiny
nectar glands at the leaf base known as
extrafloral nectaries because they are a

non-flower source of nectar. These glands are common to cherry trees. The leaves turn a golden yellow in the fall. Bitter cherry has a distinctive reddish-brown bark with pronounced lenticels. The bark may have a slight peeling appearance, often resembling a dark-colored paper birch. *Prunus* refers to cherry or plum, and *emarginata* means removed margin (a reference to the fine serrations in the leaf margins).

Quick facts about bitter cherry:

- Short-lived early-successional species
- Shade intolerant
- Common but sporadic occurrence
- Abundant white blossoms in the spring
- Red, inedible fruit in the fall

Common uses:

Traditional
- Bark: various medicinal preparations, decorative baskets, wrap/binding for implements

Other cherries

Mazzard cherry.

Bitter cherry is one of two native cherries in western Washington, the other being chokecherry (*Prunus virginiana*). Whereas bitter cherry usually grows as a tree west of the Cascades, chokecherry generally grows as a shrub. Chokecherry flowers and fruit come in larger, longer clusters than bitter cherry, its leaves are pointed, and its bark does not show the lenticels.

There is also a common, nonnative, Eurasian cherry tree, mazzard cherry (*Prunus avium*), that can occur in wooded areas. This is sometimes referred to as "wild cherry," but it should not be confused with the native bitter cherry. The leaf characteristics can provide some distinction. For instance, compared to bitter cherry, mazzard cherry has larger leaves that form a point, and its extrafloral nectaries are larger, redder, and lower on the leaf stalk. To further complicate things, mazzard cherry has naturally hybridized with bitter cherry, resulting in a hybrid known as Puget Sound cherry: *Prunus x pugetensis* (Jacobson and Zika, 2007).

13. Pacific willow
(*Salix lucida, var. lasiandra*)
Willow family (*Salicaceae*)

Several different varieties of willows
grow in western Washington. Willows
are characterized by fuzzy catkins that
emerge in the spring, as well as slender
leaves that are sometimes rounded and
sometimes form a point at the tip. While it is
easy to identify a tree as a willow, it can be difficult
to distinguish between specific species. Add subspecies, ornamentals, and
hybrids to the mix, and identification gets even trickier. Most of the native
willow species in Washington do not form trees, but rather shrubs and
thickets, usually around water, providing important wildlife habitat. The
two willow species that are most likely to reach tree heights are Pacific
willow and Scouler's willow.

Pacific willow may
be the easiest to identify,
because of its uniquely
long, narrow leaves that
taper to a sharp point,
usually with a slight curve
at the end. The leaves are
glossy green on top and
pale underneath. There

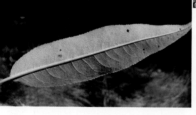

are two prominent round stipules (small leaf-like structures)
that encircle the base of each leaf

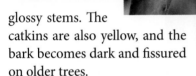

stalk. Another unique characteristic of Pacific willow leaves is that they have a collection of tiny, wart-like glands at the base of the leaf blade. Pacific willow has bright yellow buds that look like duck bills and cling closely to the glossy stems. The catkins are also yellow, and the bark becomes dark and fissured on older trees.

Male catkin.

Pacific willow is common throughout western Washington in wet areas such as streamsides, lake-shores, and wetlands. It can grow to over 50 feet (15 m) tall, making it one of the tallest willow species. Willows are shade intolerant and generally not long lived. Salicin (which is similar to aspirin) and salicylic acid can both be derived from willow bark.

Pacific willow is also known as whiplash willow, black willow, or red willow, among other common names. *Salix* means near water, *lucida* means shiny, and *lasiandra* means hairy stamens.

Quick facts about Pacific willow:

- Long, narrow leaves that taper to a sharp point
- Prominent round stipules that encircle the leaf stem
- Distinctive glands at the base of the leaf blade
- One of the tallest willows, able to reach heights of over 50 feet
- Found in wet areas

Common uses of willows in general:

Traditional
- Wood: friction fire-starter sets
- Bark: string/twine
- Shoots: baskets

14. Scouler's willow

(*Salix scouleriana*)
Willow family (*Salicaceae*)

Scouler's willow is the other willow that is likely to reach tree size, growing up to 40 feet (12 m) tall. Scouler's willow is very different from Pacific willow. Its leaves are broad and oblong, widest toward the tip (which is usually rounded or has a very slight point), and tapered at the base.

The leaves are glossy green on top and have white hairs underneath, giving the underside a waxy appearance but not as lustrous or satiny as the shrub-like Sitka willow, whose leaves are similar. The stipules (small, leaf-like structures at the base of each leaf stem) on Scouler's willow

are pointed, which can also help discriminate between it and other species that look similar. The bark of Scouler's willow has a striped appearance.

Scouler's willow can be found in wet, lowland areas. However, unlike other willows, it also grows on drier sites away from water and at higher elevations. This makes it one of the most broadly distributed willow species. *Salix* means near water, and both the common and scientific species names honor naturalist John Scouler.

Quick facts about Scouler's willow:

- Oblong leaves that are widest near the usually rounded tip
- Pointed stipules
- Grows up to 40 feet tall
- Widely distributed, including dry upland sites

Common uses of willows in general:

Traditional

- Wood: friction fire-starter sets
- Bark: string/twine
- Shoots: baskets

Similar species: Sitka willow (*Salix sitchensis*)

Another common willow that can look similar to Scouler's willow is Sitka willow. Sitka willow grows in wet areas and does not usually grow to more than 10 feet (3 m) tall. The undersides of Sitka willow leaves are much more lustrous than Scouler's willow, and Sitka willow has rounded instead of pointed stipules.

15. Pacific Madrone

(*Arbutus menziesii*)
Heath family (*Ericaceae*)

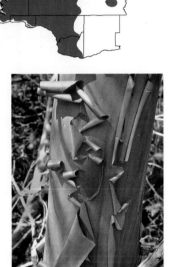

Pacific madrone, also called madrona, is one of the most distinctive Northwest trees. It has bright red bark that peels off in curls, exposing the light-colored and very smooth surface underneath. This is an example of a broad-leaved tree that is ever-green, as it keeps its thick, glossy green leaves through the winter for a total

of 1.25 years, dropping them after new spring foliage has emerged. The tree often has a twisted, irregular form, though it can also have a well-rounded canopy. Regardless of its form, it is beautiful and easy to spot and identify.

This lowland tree is typically associated with saltwater, being abundant near the coast and adorning the dry, rocky bluffs above Puget Sound and throughout the islands. It can also be found further inland, though, on exposed, rocky sites. It is drought-tolerant but easily killed by fire. It has intermediate shade tolerance. Young seedlings may actually need the protection of partial shade to get established, but the tree demands more light as it grows.

The madrone produces ornate clusters of small white flowers in the spring that look like little urns or lanterns. These flowers mature to clusters of orange-red berries that are enjoyed by wildlife but not usually consumed by people. The name madrone comes from the Spanish *madroño*, which means strawberry tree, because its fruit resembles the Mediterranean strawberry tree (*Arbutus unedo*), which is in the same genus. The genus name *Arbutus* also means

strawberry tree. The scientific species name *menziesii* honors Scottish botanist Archibald Menzies.

Madrone is vulnerable to a variety of fungal diseases. Foliar diseases cause unsightly blotches on the leaves. This is largely a cosmetic issue rather than a serious threat, and the emergence of new spring foliage will alleviate the impact. Stem diseases like madrone twig dieback and madrone canker can be more serious. Keeping the trees vigorous and avoiding injuries are the best ways to keep madrones healthy.

Quick facts about Pacific madrone:

- Distinctive, peeling bark
- A broad-leaved tree that is evergreen
- Most common near saltwater
- Intermediate shade intolerance
- Clusters of white flowers in the spring
- Orange-red berries in the fall

Common uses:

Traditional
- Leaves: medicinal infusions for colds and other ailments
- Berries: occasionally used as food

Modern
- Wood: firewood, veneer, flooring

16. Cascara
(Rhamnus purshiana)
Buckthorn family *(Rhamnaceae)*

Cascara is famous for its medicinal properties, as laxatives are derived from its bark. The bark is indeed potent, and using a stick from this tree to stir or roast food over a campfire is enough to get strong results (to the delight of pranksters). The name cascara comes from the Spanish *cáscara*, meaning bark. The scientific species name *purshiana* refers to German botanist Friedrich Pursh, while the genus name *Rhamnus* simply means buckthorn.

Cascara is a common tree found throughout western Washington. It is a small shade-tolerant tree that usually does not exceed 40 feet (12 m) in height, though it can grow taller under the right conditions. It is found on both moist and dry low-elevation sites. The bark is light brownish-gray with white patches and can look similar to red alder, with which it often grows in association. It readily sprouts from cut stumps.

The distinctive leaves will help you identify cascara. The leaves are oval with a slight

point at the end, a glossy green color, and very prominent, deep, and parallel veins. These veins become very obvious when backlit by the sun. The leaf arrangement is also distinctive, with leaves growing in lopsided umbrella-shaped clusters with the flowers and fruits in the middle. The flowers are small and light green,

maturing to dark purple berries that are enjoyed by wildlife, especially band-tailed pigeons. The leaves turn yellow in the fall, but they also can reveal more intense orange and red hues, especially around the leaf edges, when first changing in early fall.

Quick facts about cascara:

- Bark is a powerful medicinal (laxative)
- Small shade-tolerant tree
- Clusters of prominently-veined oval leaves
- Produces purple berries

Common uses:

Traditional
- Bark: laxative, dye, infusion for sores

Modern
- Bark: laxative

17. Pacific dogwood

(*Cornus nuttallii*)
Dogwood family (*Cornaceae*)

Pacific dogwood, also called western flowering dogwood, is one of the loveliest trees in western Washington forests. It has a somewhat delicate form with a narrow and often sparse crown, especially in deep shade. Pacific dogwood is shade tolerant and grows on both moist and dry sites. Similar to the yew tree, it is a species found throughout western Washington, but is not very abundant and usually occurs as sporadic individuals. Pacific dogwood has been heavily impacted by an introduced fungal disease called dogwood anthracnose, which causes lesions on the leaves and cankers on the stem and branches.

Dogwoods make themselves known in the spring, emerging from the background with showy structures that resemble white flowers. This can be particularly noticeable along forest edges. The flowers are actually very small clusters in the middle of what appear to be large white petals. These "petals" are actually modified leaves called bracts. The flowers form rounded clusters of

The flowers form the drupelets of an aggregate fruit.

berry-like aggregate fruits that turn red in early fall and are enjoyed by wildlife, but are not eaten by people.

Pacific dogwood leaves are elliptical and come to a distinct point at the tip. Pronounced veins curve parallel to the leaf margins. The leaves

turn shades of pink and red in the fall. The bark is thin, smooth, and brownish-gray. Dogwood will sprout from cut stumps. The name dogwood comes from *dagwood*, as the dogwood's hard wood makes it suitable for skewers or *dags*. The scientific species name *nuttallii* is for naturalist Thomas Nuttall, who helped to identify it as its own species distinct from flowering dogwood (*Cornus florida*). The genus name *Cornus* means hard, in reference to the wood.

There are two other native dogwoods in western Washington. Red osier dogwood (*Cornus stolonifera*) is a woody shrub, and bunchberry (*Cornus unalaschkensis*) is an herbaceous groundcover.

Quick facts about Pacific dogwood:

- Widespread but not common
- Slender, delicate form
- Shade tolerant
- Small flowers surrounded by showy white bracts in the spring
- Red fruits in the fall
- Highly susceptible to dogwood anthracnose

Common uses:

Traditional
- Wood: implements, small discs for a gambling game
- Bark: sometimes used in infusions

18. Paper birch

(*Betula papyrifera*)
Birch family (*Betulaceae*)

Paper birch is most recognizable by its bark that peels off in thin paper-like sheets. This bark is usually white, but

the color can range all the way to dark brown, especially in younger trees, and has pronounced horizontal lenticels similar to bitter cherry. In fact, dark-colored birch bark can be difficult to distinguish from that of bitter cherry. The waxy bark is both waterproof and flammable, making it suitable for a variety of uses, from canoes to a fire starter. *Betula* means pitch, and *papyrifera* means paper-bearing.

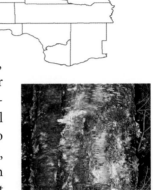

The bark of younger trees may appear dark, resembling bitter cherry.

Paper birch has ovate leaves that taper to a distinct point at the end. The leaves turn golden yellow in the fall. The male and female flowers are

catkins similar to alder. However, female birch catkins disintegrate at maturity, not becoming persistent and woody like alder.

Paper birch has a wide native range stretching from Alaska to Newfoundland, with most of its range in Canada. On the west coast, the range dips down to include the northern part of western Washington. It is prolific across Whatcom County, often growing together with grand fir. Its occurrence drops off sharply as you go south, with its native range ending right around Seattle. Paper birch is found in cool, moist, low-elevation areas. It is a shade-intolerant pioneer species that grows on disturbed sites with exposed mineral soil. It can also sprout from cut stumps. It is a medium-sized tree that usually grows to between 30 and 70 feet (10–20 m) tall and up to 2 feet (0.6 m) in diameter. It is shallow rooted and does not form a taproot. Its lifespan is approximately 100 years.

Quick facts about paper birch:

- Bark peels off in waterproof sheets
- Grows natively in the northern part of western Washington
- Shade intolerant
- Grows in cool, moist areas

Common uses:

Traditional (more by interior than coastal peoples)
- Wood: firewood
- Bark: fire starter, canoes, baskets, roofing

Modern
- Wood: firewood

19. Oregon white oak

(*Quercus garryana*)
Beech family (*Fagaceae*)

Oregon white oak, also called the Garry oak, is the only native oak in Washington. It grows in dry, open grassland areas, particularly in the prairies and savannahs of the South Puget Trough. It is very common in the prairies around Joint Base Lewis-McChord. You will also find it further north, in dry rain shadow areas like Whidbey Island and the San Juans. The city of Oak Harbor was named for this tree. *Quercus* means oak, and *garryana* refers to Nicholas Garry, a deputy governor of the Hudson's Bay Company and a benefactor of Scottish botanist and Pacific Northwest explorer David Douglas.

Oregon white oak is a beautiful tree with a rounded, spreading

canopy. The leaves have seven to nine rounded lobes, and are a deep, glossy green on top. The bark is gray with narrow fissures. The tree also produces an acorn that has a shallow cap, making it one of the few species in western Washington that yields hard mast. This is an important food source for wildlife. Oregon white oak forms a deep taproot, and it is very wind resistant. It is intolerant of shade, larger specimens are fire resistant, and it can sprout from cut stumps.

Native oak woodlands or savannahs have greatly declined in Washington, with only a fraction of this ecosystem remaining compared to pre-European settlement. Without the regular burning that was done by Native Americans, dense conifer forests tend to take over these previously open oak communities. Many of these areas have also been replaced by urban development and farmland. Projects have been launched to restore oak/prairie ecosystems by removing Douglas-fir and reintroducing prescribed fire.

Quick facts about Oregon white oak:

- Grows in dry, open grasslands
- Especially prevalent in the South Puget Trough, north Whidbey Island, and the San Juan Islands
- Produces an acorn important for wildlife
- Intolerant of shade
- Oak savannahs are in decline due to development and lack of burning

Common uses:

Traditional
- Wood: firewood, digging sticks, and other implements
- Acorns: food
- Bark: used in infusions to treat tuberculosis

Modern
- Wood: firewood, lumber (historically), fence posts

20. Oregon ash
(*Fraxinus latifolia*)
Olive family (*Oleaceae*)

Oregon ash is found in lowland areas in the southwestern part of the state, from about Tacoma southward. It grows in wet habitats, such as bottomlands and swamps. Having only moderate shade tolerance, it prefers open areas. It is resistant to wind and flooding, giving it an advantage in wet areas. Like the more widespread ash trees in the eastern United States, Oregon ash has hard, dense wood. It can live up to 250 years, and it readily sprouts from cut stumps.

Oregon ash has several readily distinguishable features. It has pinnately compound leaves, meaning that a single leaf comprises multiple leaflets growing in two rows along the leaf stalk. An Oregon ash leaf has two to four opposite pairs of leaflets, with a single leaflet at the end. The scientific species name *latifolia* means broad-leaved, while the genus name *Fraxinus* simply refers to an ash tree. Deer and elk will feed on the leaves.

The rough bark has crisscrossing furrows, giving it a woven or braided appearance. Oregon ash has separate male and female trees (i.e., it is dioecious), with only the females bearing fruit, which are clusters of samaras. Unlike bigleaf maple which has samaras fused together in pairs, Oregon ash samaras are individually attached. Ash samaras have a curve to them, giving them a distinctive canoe shape. The seeds are an important source of hard mast for birds and squirrels.

Samaras.

Quick facts about Oregon ash:

- Grows in the southwestern part of the state
- Grows in moist to very wet areas
- Intermediate shade tolerance
- Resistant to wind and flooding
- Has pinnately compound leaves and single samaras
- Important food source for wildlife

Common uses:

Traditional
- Wood: canoe paddles

Modern
- Wood: firewood

21. Pacific crabapple

(*Malus fusca*)
Rose family (*Rosaceae*)

Pacific crabapple, also called Oregon crabapple, is Washington's native wild apple tree. Like yew or dogwood, this tree is found throughout the western Washington lowlands, but not as commonly as other species. It is most often found growing near water, such as along saltwater shore- lines or the edges of lakes, bogs, or ponds. Pacific crabapple can be either a large, thicket-form- ing woody shrub or a small tree of 30–40 feet (9–12 m) tall. It is slow-growing and often has a twisted, gnarled form. The wood is hard and dense.

The leaves of this tree are variable and can have one or more lobes. Some leaves may form a mitten shape with a prominent thumb. A distinct characteristic of this tree is that its

Branches and twigs have spikes.

small twigs and branches are armed with thorn-like spikes, though the spikes are not terribly sharp. The crabapple produces fragrant blossoms in the spring, which mature into small fruits that are edible, but tart. These fruits were eaten by native peoples, and they are also a food source for wildlife. The bark is fissured and platy. *Malus* means apple, and *fusca* means dark brown.

Quick facts about Pacific crabapple:

- Grows near water
- Forms a small tree or a shrubby thicket
- Twigs and branches have thorn-like spikes
- Produces small, edible fruits

Common uses:

Traditional
- Wood: wedges, prongs for seal spears
- Fruit: food
- Bark: various medicinal uses, including infusions, wound applications, and eyewash

Modern
- Fruit: food, pectin

Similar species: Black hawthorn (*Crataegus douglasii*)

Another native species with similar characteristics of spiked branches and small fruits is black hawthorn. Both are members of the rose family. The spikes on hawthorn are much sharper than crabapple.

High-elevation Species

22. Mountain hemlock

(*Tsuga mertensiana*)
Pine family (*Pinaceae*)

Common throughout the Cascade and Olympic Mountains, mountain hemlock grows above 3,000 feet (915 m) and all the way to timberline, so you can find it at most of the mountain passes as well as places like Mount Rainier, Mount Baker, and Hurricane Ridge. *Tsuga* is derived from the Japanese word meaning mother tree, while *mertensiana* refers to German botanist Karl Mertens.

Mountain hemlock is a shade-tolerant tree that takes many forms depending on elevation and conditions, ranging from a large, stately tree to a stunted or even twisted, shrub-like form, called the krummholz formation, in more extreme subalpine environments. *Krummholz* is German for twisted wood. Mountain hemlock has a droopy top like the western hemlock, although the top of some trees can appear windswept and flattened. Mountain hemlock is flexible, which allows it to tolerate heavy snow loads.

The mountain hemlock has short needles similar to its low-elevation cousin the western hemlock. However, compared to the flat sprays of western hemlock, mountain hemlock needles are arranged spirally around the twig, giving it a star-like

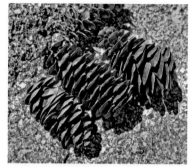

appearance when looking down the branch. This needle arrangement gives the foliage a bushy appearance. A close inspection will reveal that the leaves are attached by little woody stems, similar to a spruce. On mature trees, the bark is dark and deeply-furrowed, sometimes even resembling Douglas-fir. The cones have a color and texture similar to western hemlock but are longer at 1.5–3 inches (4–8 cm).

Quick facts about mountain hemlock:

- Common throughout the mountain regions
- Top droops like western hemlock
- Needles are similar to western hemlock but spirally arranged
- Can form a large, robust tree or take on a twisted, shrub-like form

Common uses

Traditional
- Boughs: sleeping mats, brushes
- Other uses similar to western hemlock

Modern
- Wood: limited lumber use

23. Pacific silver fir

(*Abies amabilis*)
Pine family (*Pinaceae*)

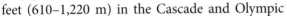

Pacific silver fir, also known as amabilis fir, is one of several true firs that grow at higher elevations in western Washington. Pacific silver fir is a mid-elevation species, typically growing between 2,000 and 4,000 feet (610–1,220 m) in the Cascade and Olympic Mountains, as well as the Black and Willapa Hills. In some places on the west side of the Olympic Peninsula, though, you may see Pacific silver fir all the way down to sea level.

The needles of Pacific silver fir are similar to its low-elevation cousin, the grand fir: they are glossy green on top, with two pronounced white stomatal bands on the bottom. These stomatal bands give the underside a beautiful silvery shimmer, which gives rise to both the common and scientific names (*Abies* means tall or rising, and *amabilis* means beautiful). Even the bark of this tree is a silver gray, smooth with resin blisters on

younger trees, and becoming more platy on older, larger trees. It produces decent-quality wood.

Pacific silver fir can be distinguished from grand fir by the arrangement of its needles. Unlike the grand fir's flat, two-ranked needle arrangement, the Pacific silver fir stacks its

needles in a bushy pattern on top of the twig, tilting forward toward the branch tip rather than sticking out perpendicular like grand fir.

Like other true firs, Pacific silver fir has upright, cylindrical cones that grow at the top of the tree and shed layer by layer. Pacific silver fir cones are 3–6 inches (8–15 cm) long. Pacific silver fir is extremely shade tolerant, even more so than mountain hemlock, allowing it to dominate mid-elevation forests over time in the absence of disturbance. Native American uses of Pacific silver fir were similar to those of grand fir, with the two species used somewhat interchangeably.

Quick facts about Pacific silver fir:

- Common at mid elevations throughout the mountain regions
- Branch undersides have silvery shimmer
- Needles stacked on top of the twig and tilted forward
- Very shade tolerant

Common uses:

Traditional
- Similar to grand fir

Modern
- Wood: dimensional lumber

24. Noble fir

(*Abies procera*)
Pine family (*Pinaceae*)

Noble fir is another mid-elevation
true fir, growing between 2,000 and
5,000 feet (610–1,525 m). It grows in
the Cascades from about Snoqualmie
Pass southward. In these areas you will
find it growing together with Pacific silver
fir and mountain hemlock. There are also some
isolated stands in the Willapa Hills area.

Noble fir stand near Mount St. Helens.

The distinguishing characteristic of noble fir needles is four stomatal
bands: two on top, and two on the bottom. The needles also make an "L"
or hockey-stick shape coming off of the twig. The stomatal bands on both
sides of the needles give the foliage a dull, bluish appearance. This blue tint

helps noble fir stick out from the greener Pacific silver fir and mountain hemlock with which it often grows. A great example is found along the road to Paradise at Mount Rainier, where good examples of most of our high-elevation species grow together. Another good place to find noble fir is along the road to Johnston Ridge at Mount St. Helens. After the 1980 eruption, noble fir was replanted in the higher elevations of the blast zone, creating pure stands with a striking appearance.

Younger bark is smooth with resin blisters, becoming platy on older, larger trees. Noble fir has particularly spectacular cones with a light tan color that really stands out. Like all true firs, noble fir cones are upright, cylindrical, form at the top of the tree, and fall apart at maturity. Noble fir cones are particularly large, ranging from 4–6 inches (10–15 cm) long. If you look carefully at noble fir cones, you will see unique thin bracts that stick out from between the cone scales.

True to its name, noble fir is a tall, stately tree, reaching heights of up to 260 feet (79 m). This is greater than any other true fir, and it is reflected in the tree's scientific species name, with *procera* meaning tall. Noble fir is the most shade intolerant of the true firs in Washington.

Noble fir has high-quality wood, with a high strength-to-weight ratio like Sitka spruce. Early lumbermen sometimes marketed it as larch, since the wood of true firs was generally viewed as inferior. Noble fir is a popular Christmas tree.

Quick facts about noble fir:

- Mid-elevations species
- Grows from Snoqualmie Pass southward
- Needles have two stomatal bands on each side, giving a blue appearance
- Large cones
- Shade intolerant
- High-quality wood

Common uses:

Modern
- Wood: dimensional lumber
- Christmas trees

25. Subalpine fir
(*Abies lasiocarpa*)
Pine family (*Pinaceae*)

Subalpine fir is a mid- to high-elevation tree that grows from 2,000 feet
(610 m) all the way up to timberline,
and is one of the most commonly found
trees at timberline. This denizen of the
high country is found throughout the Cascade
and Olympic Mountains.

Subalpine fir is easily
recognized by its nar-
row, spire-like crown
that sheds snow. In the
more extreme conditions
at timberline, you'll find
clumps of small, wind-
swept trees or even the
shrubby, twisted krumm-
holz form. Its delicate
appearance belies its har-

diness, as this tree can hold
its own in harsh mountain
conditions. Subalpine fir
is relatively shade tolerant,
though not as much as Pacific
silver fir or mountain hemlock. Subalpine fir can reproduce by seed and also vegetatively by layering—where
low, spreading branches get
pressed against the ground,
put down roots, and send up
a leader to form a new tree.
This creates clonal clumps.

Subalpine fir grows together with other high-elevation true firs, but you can distinguish it by its needles, which have three stomatal bands: two on the bottom and one on the top. This gives the foliage a glaucous appearance, but not as much as noble fir. Subalpine fir has gray-brown bark which becomes fissured on older, larger trees. Subalpine fir does not have good quality wood. Native Americans had several uses for it, including using the resin as a chewing gum and a salve for wounds.

The bark is smooth and blistery on young trees.

The bark of older trees is rough and platy.

Like all true firs, subalpine fir cones are upright, cylindrical, form at the top of the tree, and fall apart at maturity. The cones of the subalpine fir are 2–4 inches (5–10 cm) long, which is small compared to other true firs, but they are some of the most stunning because of their deep indigo to purple color. The cones are very resinous. The scientific species name *lasiocarpa* means rough cones.

Quick facts about subalpine fir:

- Mid-high elevations species that is common at timberline
- Narrow, spire-like crown sheds snow
- Needles have one stomatal band on top and two underneath
- Cones are a deep indigo to purple color
- Shade tolerant

Common uses:

Traditional
- Resin: chewing gum, salve

26. Alaska yellow cedar

(*Callitropsis nootkatensis*)
Cypress family (*Cupressaceae*)

Like the western redcedar, Alaska yellow cedar is not a true cedar, but is a
"false cedar" that is part of the cypress
family. Also like western redcedar, it is
one of the hardiest and longest-lived
Northwest trees. Alaska yellow cedar is also known
as Nootka cypress, and has several other common names. It is a mid- to
high-elevation species, growing from 2,000 to over 7,000 feet (610–2,125
m) throughout the Olympic and western Cascade Mountains. It will also
grow down to sea level further north in British Columbia and Alaska.

In its most classic form, Alaska yellow
cedar has a weepy appearance with very
droopy branches. Even so, it can sometimes be difficult to distinguish between
Alaska yellow cedar and western redcedar
at mid-elevation where their ranges over-
lap. The overlapping scale foliage is very
similar between the two species, especially
on top. But if you turn over the Alaska yellow cedar foliage, you'll see that it does not
have the prominent white waxy areas that
the western redcedar does.

The underside of Alaskan yellow cedar.

The bark of mature
Alaska yellow cedar
comes in strips like
western redcedar, but
they are wider, block-
ier, and lighter in color.
Younger bark may be
more brown and flaky.
Alaska yellow cedar
produces very small

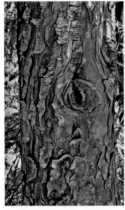  

Bark of a younger tree.   Bark of a mature tree.

cones that are approximately 1/3 inch (8 mm) in diameter, similar to western redcedar. However, Alaska yellow cedar cones are more spherical.

This shade-tolerant species is often planted as an ornamental at low elevations. Its strong, durable, decay-resistant, straight-grained wood is valuable for lumber and woodworking. It is particularly prized in Japan, where it is imported from North America. Native Americans used Alaska yellow cedar wood for paddles, bows, dishes, and other implements.

Quick facts about Alaska yellow cedar:

- Mid-high elevations species
- Droopy branches
- Similar appearance to western redcedar
- Shade tolerant
- Prized wood

Common uses:

Traditional
- Wood: paddles, bows, dishes, implements

Modern
- Wood: dimensional lumber, timbers, siding, shingles, shakes

Identity crisis

Many species are known by a variety of different common names, and Alaska yellow cedar is no exception. However, rarely is there as much disagreement among botanists over a scientific name as there is with this species. It has been known by four different scientific names: *Cupressus nootkatensis*, *Chamaecyparis nootkatensis*, *Xanthocyparis nootkatensis*, and *Callitropsis nootkatensis*. As of this writing, *Callitropsis* seems to be favored, but the nomenclature still does not appear to be fully resolved and there is talk about returning to the original *Cupressus*. Callitropsis means similar to the *Callitris* genus (which means beautiful), and nootkatensis refers to Nootka Sound on the west coast of Vancouver Island.

27. Engelmann spruce

(*Picea engelmannii*)
Pine family (*Pinaceae*)

Engelmann spruce is a mid- to
high-elevation species that grows
from 1,000 feet (305 m) up to the
timberline. It is much more common
east of the Cascade Crest, and it is only
occasionally found on the west slopes and in
certain parts of the Olympics. It tends to prefer cold,
moist environments. The accompanying photos were taken along the
road to Sunrise at Mount Rainier.

Like its low-elevation cousin
the Sitka spruce, Engelmann
spruce needles are sharp and grow
on little wooden pegs. Unlike
the Sitka spruce, though, the
Engelmann spruce needles are not
flat but are four-sided and will roll
between your fingers. They also
have a blue tint to them, making this tree fairly easy to spot. The bark
is also very different from the Sitka spruce. Engelmann spruce has thin,

platy, or scaly bark that looks like alli-
gator skin. Engelmann spruce cones are
1–2.5 inches (2.5–6 cm) long and look
similar to Sitka spruce, except the scales
do not lie as flat, giving them a bushier
appearance.

Engelmann spruce is shade tolerant, but not as much as its high-
elevation cohort, the subalpine fir. It is
particularly vulnerable to windthrow.
It is not a commercial species in western Washington, but in other parts of
its range it is valued for its high-quality pulp. The genus name *Picea* means

Engelmann spruce cones.

pitch-producing, and both the common and scientific names refer to German-American botanist George Engelmann. Spruce means "from Prussia."

Quick facts about Engelmann spruce:

- Mid-high elevations species
- More common in eastern Washington but occasionally found west of the Cascade Crest
- Foliage has a blue tint

28. Whitebark pine

(*Pinus albicaulis*)
Pine family (*Pinaceae*)

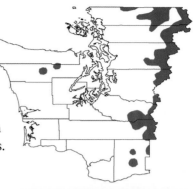

Whitebark pine is truly a high-elevation species, growing from 4,500 feet
(1,370 m) up to the timberline in both
the Olympic and Cascade Mountains.

It is slow-growing. It can become a
tall, straight tree, but because of its
extreme habitat range, you often find
it in more twisted, stunted, or even
krummholz forms. Nonetheless, these
windswept trees are some of the loveliest in the state.

It is a white pine, so it has needles
in clusters of five like its low-elevation cousin the western white pine.
Whitebark pine needles are shorter

and thicker than western white pine. As its name implies, the bark of the whitebark pine is a light grayish-white. Its scientific name, *Pinus albicaulis*, means pine with a white stem. If you are lucky enough to find a cone, they are a beautiful deep purple, very similar in color (but not in shape or form) to subalpine fir cones. A bird, the Clark's nutcracker

(*Nucifraga columbiana*), and squirrels crack open the cones and feed on and disperse the seeds.

The whitebark pine is becoming more rare in Washington. Being a white pine, it is a victim of the exotic white pine blister rust disease (see the western white pine section). It is also becoming more subject to bark beetle attacks due to a warming climate. It has been considered for listing under the Endangered Species Act. The Sunrise area at Mount Rainier is a good place to find this species. Whitebark pine is shade intolerant.

Quick facts about whitebark pine:

- High elevation species
- Five-needle pine with white bark
- Clark's nutcrackers particularly enjoy feeding on the seeds
- Becoming rare due to climate change and an exotic disease

Common uses:

Traditional:
- Seeds: food

Isolated Populations

29. Ponderosa pine

(*Pinus ponderosa*)
Pine family (*Pinaceae*)

Ponderosa pine is very abundant east of the Cascades, even typ-
ifying that part of the state. It is rare
to find it growing natively in western
Washington, though. The largest population of western ponderosa pine is in the
Joint Base Lewis-McChord area between Olympia
and Tacoma. There are also very localized remnants of this population
in communities like Spanaway.
These pines are associates of the
Oregon white oak and were part
of the fire-maintained prairie
ecosystem in the South Puget
Trough area. Ponderosa pine was
named such by Scottish botanist
and Pacific Northwest explorer
David Douglas because of its large
size (*ponderosa* meaning large or
weighty).

Ponderosa pine has longer needles than the other native pines in
Washington, and most often they are in bun-
dles of three, though occasionally you will find
bundles of two. The bark is distinctive and
different from the other
native pines. On mature
trees the color ranges from
light gray to orange. It will
be flaky, with patterns that
look similar to jigsaw puz-
zle pieces when viewed up
close. If you put your nose
up to it, you may smell a
hint of vanilla. Ponderosa

pine has open, egg-shaped cones that are 3–6 inches (8–15 cm) long and are roughly the size of a small adult fist. They have little thorns or "prickles" at the ends of the cone scales.

Ponderosa pine is a major commercial lumber species in eastern Washington but not in western Washington because of its scarcity. Ponderosa pine is shade intolerant. It is tolerant of drought, though, and it can form a deep taproot that helps it survive on extreme sites. Like its prairie cohort the Oregon white oak, ponderosa pine is adapted to fire. Its thick bark is very fire resistant, allowing mature ponderosa pines to withstand frequent, low-intensity fires. The exclusion of fire in the south Puget Sound prairie ecosystem has allowed the formerly open savannah-like stands of oak and ponderosa pine to become overgrown with other conifers like Douglas-fir.

Quick facts about ponderosa pine:

- Very common in eastern Washington, but rare in western Washington
- Found with Oregon white oak in prairie areas of the South Puget Trough
- Usually three needles per bundle
- Shade intolerant
- Drought and fire tolerant

Common uses:

Traditional
- Wood: firewood, building materials, and various tools and implements
- Inner bark and seeds: food
- Pitch: sealant, salves, glue, chewing gum
- Needles: boiled to make a medicinal tea

Modern
- Important lumber species throughout its range, but too rare in western Washington for commercial use

30. Quaking aspen

(*Populus tremuloides*)
Willow family (*Salicaceae*)

Quaking aspen, also called trembling aspen, is typically found at high elevations east of the Cascade Crest. On the west it is known to be native in the North Cascades, in small localized pockets at the southern end of Hood Canal, south of Tumwater, and possibly in eastern Skamania County.

Aspen is in the willow family, in the same genus as black cottonwood. Its leaves have some similarities to black cottonwood, but a little shorter and rounder. What is really distinctive about an aspen leaf, though, is its flat stem, in contrast to cottonwood leaves that have round stems. This flat stem causes the aspen leaves to flutter in the slightest wind, earning it the quaking or trembling appellation. The scientific name *Populous tremuloides* means poplar that trembles. The leaves turn bright gold in the fall.

Aspen has smooth cream-color bark, with scars that look like eyes. Similar to its cousin the black cottonwood, aspen is very shade intolerant. Unlike cottonwood, though, aspen is a relatively small tree, only

growing to approximately 80 feet (24 m) tall. Although it produces seeds (with cottony tufts, similar to black cottonwood), it is particularly well-known for its ability to propagate vegetatively by suckers from its extensive root system, which creates colonies of aspen that are all clones of the same tree.

Quick facts about quaking aspen:

- More common at high elevations in eastern Washington
- Isolated populations in the North Cascades, the southern end of Hood Canal, and south of Tumwater
- Flat-stemmed leaves cause the leaves to "quake" in the breeze
- Aggressive root suckering creates clonal colonies

31. Seaside juniper

(*Juniperus maritima*)
Cypress family (*Cupressaceae*)

Seaside juniper is a dry-site species that used to be thought of as a rare western Washington occurrence of Rocky Mountain juniper (*Juniperus scopulorum*). However, a study published in 2007 concluded that it is a genetically distinct species (Adams, R.P. 2007. *Juniperus maritima*, the seaside juniper, a new species from Puget Sound, North America. *Phytologia* 89(3):263-283). Also called Puget Sound Juniper, it grows along the northern shores of Puget Sound in very dry areas such as the San Juan Islands. There are also some localized populations in the rain shadow area of the northeast Olympic Mountains. A good place to reliably find seaside juniper is at Washington Park on the tip of Fidalgo Island in Anacortes. *Juniperus* means evergreen and *maritima* means by the sea.

Juniper is in the Cypress family, just like the false cedars. It has two types of foliage. The foliage on young trees is composed of short, prickly

Youthful foliage is short and prickly.

Mature foliage with overlapping scales.

spikes. On older trees the foliage is composed of overlapping scales. Like other junipers, it produces small blue berries, which are not actually berries but rather modified cone scales. "Berries" from the seaside juniper's shrubby relative, the common juniper (*Juniperus communis*), are known for their use as a flavoring in gin. Seaside juniper is dioecious, with separate male and female plants, with only the females producing berries. The brown-gray outer bark has strips similar to western redcedar or Alaska

yellow cedar. Seaside juniper often has a gnarled or even shrubby form along windswept bluffs, but it can also grow as a relatively straight, symmetrical tree.

Seaside juniper has intermediate shade tolerance, being more tolerant when young but demanding more light as it grows.

Quick facts about seaside juniper:

- Formerly thought to be a western Washington occurrence of Rocky Mountain juniper
- Grows on dry, rocky sites in the north Puget Sound and northeast Olympic Peninsula areas
- Produces blue juniper "berries"

32. Golden chinkapin

(*Chrysolepis chrysophylla*)
Beech family (*Fagaceae*)

Golden chinkapin (also spelled chin-
quapin) is present but rare in western
Washington, which is the very northern tip of its range. There are known to
be isolated populations in the southwest
Hood Canal area, and also in the Wind River
area east of Vancouver near the Columbia River
Gorge. It is much more common in Oregon and California.

Like madrone, golden
chinkapin is a broad-leaved
tree that is evergreen. The
thick, leathery leaves are
slender and pointed, widest
near the middle, and tapered
at both ends. They are dark
green on top, but golden
underneath, which makes
this tree easy to identify,
and is also how it got its name.
Chrysolepis means golden
scales and *chrysophylla* means
golden leaves. Chinkapin can
grow as a tree or a large shrub.
It has intermediate shade toler-
ance, with the shrub form having higher tolerance. It readily sprouts from
the stump after fire or cutting. It can tolerate dry, nutrient-poor conditions.

Chinkapin has erect clusters of white flowers that have a strong, musky
odor. The distinctive fruit is a nut contained within a spiny husk, similar to a chestnut, which is eaten by birds and squirrels. The spines on the

husk are needle-sharp. The bark is brown and fissured.

Quick facts about golden chinkapin:

- Isolated populations near Hood Canal and Wind River
- Evergreen leaves are golden underneath
- Produces erect clusters of white flowers and a distinctive spiny fruit
- Can grow as a tree or large shrub

Species Lists

By family

Beech family (*Fagaceae*)
- Golden chinkapin (*Chrysolepis chrysophylla*)
- Oregon white oak (*Quercus garryana*)

Birch family (*Betulaceae*)
- Paper birch (*Betula papyrifera*)
- Red alder (*Alnus rubra*)

Buckthorn family (*Rhamnaceae*)
- Cascara (*Rhamnus purshiana*)

Cypress family (*Cupressaceae*)
- Alaska yellow cedar (*Callitropsis nootkatensis*)
- Seaside juniper (*Juniperus maritima*)
- Western redcedar (*Thuja plicata*)

Dogwood family (*Cornaceae*)
- Pacific dogwood (*Cornus nuttallii*)

Heath family (*Ericaceae*)
- Pacific madrone (*Arbutus menziesii*)

Maple family (*Aceraceae*)
- Bigleaf maple (*Acer macrophyllum*)

Olive family (*Oleaceae*)
- Oregon ash (*Fraxinus latifolia*)

Pine family (*Pinaceae*)
- Douglas-fir (*Pseudotsuga menziesii*)
- Engelmann spruce (*Picea engelmannii*)
- Grand fir (*Abies grandis*)
- Lodgepole/shore pine (*Pinus contorta*)
- Mountain hemlock (*Tsuga mertensiana*)
- Noble fir (*Abies procera*)
- Pacific silver fir (*Abies amabilis*)
- Ponderosa pine (*Pinus ponderosa*)
- Sitka spruce (*Picea sitchensis*)
- Subalpine fir (*Abies lasiocarpa*)
- Western hemlock (*Tsuga heterophylla*)
- Western white pine (*Pinus monticola*)
- Whitebark pine (*Pinus albicaulis*)

Rose family (*Rosaceae*)
- Bitter cherry (*Prunus emarginata*)
- Pacific crabapple (*Malus fusca*)

Willow family (*Salicaceae*)
- Black cottonwood (*Populus trichocarpa*)
- Pacific willow (*Salix lucida, var. lasiandra*)
- Quaking aspen (*Populus tremuloides*)
- Scouler's willow (*Salix scouleriana*)

Yew family (*Taxaceae*)
- Pacific yew (*Taxus brevifolia*)

By shade tolerance

Very intolerant

- Black cottonwood
- Lodgepole/shore pine
- Quaking aspen
- Red alder

Intolerant

- Bitter cherry
- Douglas-fir
- Noble fir
- Oregon white oak
- Paper birch
- Pacific willow
- Ponderosa pine
- Whitebark pine

Intermediate

- Golden chinkapin
- Oregon ash
- Pacific crabapple
- Pacific madrone
- Scouler's willow
- Seaside juniper
- Western white pine

Tolerant

- Alaska yellow cedar
- Bigleaf maple
- Cascara
- Engelmann spruce
- Grand fir
- Mountain hemlock
- Pacific dogwood
- Sitka spruce
- Subalpine fir

Very tolerant

- Western hemlock
- Western redcedar
- Pacific silver fir
- Pacific yew

Site and disease tolerances of lowland species

The species indicated are *generally* more tolerant *relative* to other species. Tolerances in specific situations depend on both the extent and combination of site factors.

Species tolerant of wet sites

- Bigleaf maple
- Black cottonwood
- Lodgepole pine
- Oregon ash*
- Pacific crabapple
- Pacific willow*
- Red alder
- Western redcedar

*Particularly wet-tolerant

Species tolerant of dry sites

- Cascara
- Douglas-fir
- Grand fir
- Oregon white oak*
- Pacific dogwood
- Pacific madrone*
- Shore pine

*Particularly drought-tolerant

Species tolerant of nutrient-poor sites

- Bitter cherry
- Lodgepole/shore pine
- Pacific madrone
- Red alder
- Western redcedar

Species tolerant of cold sites (e.g., frost pockets)

- Lodgepole pine
- Paper birch
- Western white pine

Wind-resistant species

While these species tend to resist windthrow more than others, wind firmness is ultimately more a function of the site (e.g., topography, soil depth, soil saturation, presence of root disease, etc.) than the species.

- Douglas-fir
- Oregon ash
- Oregon white oak
- Pacific madrone
- Western redcedar
- Western white pine

Root disease-resistant species

While these species tend to be relatively resistant to root diseases (or immune), resistance to root disease ultimately depends on the specific disease, site conditions, and tree vigor.

- Hardwood species
- Lodgepole pine
- Western redcedar
- Western white pine

Glossary

Advanced regeneration—trees that establish in the understory under an existing canopy.

Angiosperm—a plant with seeds enclosed in an ovary (fruit). The word is from the Greek for "seeds within a vessel." Broad-leaved trees are angiosperms.

Aril—a fleshy seed covering.

Bark—the protective outermost layer of a tree stem.

Bract—a specialized, leaf-like structure associated with flowers or cone scales on some trees.

Broad-leaved tree—non cone-bearing tree such as an alder, maple, or oak that is characterized by broad, usually (but not always) deciduous leaves. Also referred to as a "hardwood" tree. Broad-leaved trees are angiosperms.

Burl—an uncontrolled woody growth on the side of a tree analogous to a tumor.

Cambium—a thin layer of actively dividing (i.e., meristematic) cells found between the xylem and the phloem of a tree stem and responsible for generating new xylem and phloem tissue.

Coarse woody debris—fallen logs on the forest floor.

Compound leaf—a leaf composed of individual leaflets (each of which may resemble a separate leaf) connected to a single stalk.

Coppice—a group of trees grown by allowing cut stumps to re-sprout, or the act of cutting trees for the purpose of growing a coppice.

Canopy—the upper vegetative layers of a forest, formed by the crowns of the trees.

Catkin—an elongated, cylindrical cluster of flowers.

Cone scales—the individual plates/segments that form a seed cone.

Conifer—a cone-bearing, usually (but not always) evergreen tree such as a spruce, fir, cedar, or pine. Also referred to as a "softwood" tree. Conifers are gymnosperms.

Crown—the leaves and branches of a tree.

Deciduous—a plant that keeps its leaves for only one growing season.

Deltoid—triangular.

Dioecious—having male and female flower parts on separate plants.

Disturbance—an event that disrupts the cycle of forest development. A stand-replacing disturbance is one that kills most of the trees in a stand, allowing a new stand to initiate. Examples include fire, windstorms, floods, landslides, logging, and volcanic eruptions.

Endophyte—an organism that lives within another organism (e.g., a microorganism living within the tissue of a plant) without harming (i.e., not parasitic), and sometimes actually benefitting, the host.

Epiphyte—a plant that grows on top of another plant without harming or taking resources from it (i.e., not parasitic).

Evergreen—a plant that keeps its leaves for more than one year, thus maintaining leaf cover year-round.

Extrafloral nectary—a small, knobby, nectar-secreting gland at the base of a leaf (e.g., on cherry trees).

Fascicle—a bundle of needles on a pine tree (the number of needles per fascicle is species-specific).

Fluted—having distinct ridges.

Forest development—how a new forest stand initiates following a major disturbance and progresses, in the absence of disturbance, through open, closed, and complex structure formations.

Genus—a taxonomic subgroup of similar species, and the first word in a species' two-word scientific or botanical name.

Glaucous—having a light bluish-gray coating.

Gymnosperm—a plant with seeds that are not enclosed in an ovary (fruit). The word is from the Greek for "naked seeds." Conifers are gymnosperms.

Hardwood—a term that refers to broad-leaved trees which, in general, have denser wood than conifers.

Heartwood—the darker, inner portion of a tree stem's xylem composed of dead cells that no longer function for water transport.

Krummholz—the twisted, low-growing, shrubby form that trees sometimes take at high elevations near timberline. The word means "twisted wood" in German.

Layering—a form of vegetative reproduction where the lower branches of a tree get pressed against the ground, put down roots, and send up a leader to form a new tree.

Leader—the vertically growing shoot at the top of the tree where height growth of the main stem occurs.

Leaflet—an individual segment (that may itself looks like a separate leaf) of a compound leaf.

Lenticel—an air-exchange pore on the stem of the tree, usually in the shape of a short, horizontal line.

Lobe—a distinct pointed or rounded protrusion that forms the overall shape of a leaf.

Margin—the edge of a leaf.

Mast—tree and shrub fruits, including hard mast (e.g., nuts and acorns) and soft mast (e.g., berries).

Monoecious—having both male and female flower parts on the same plant.

Nutrients—dissolved chemicals like nitrogen, phosphorous, and potassium that are necessary for tree growth.

Ovate—broader at the base than at the tip (egg-shaped).

Overstory—the uppermost vegetative layer of a forest.

Pendant cone—a cone that hangs down from a branch like a necklace pendant.

Phenotype—the physical appearance of an organism.

Phloem—the living tissue that forms the inner bark of a tree (between the cambium and the outer bark) and is responsible for taking the sugars produced in the leaves through photosynthesis and transporting them to the roots and other parts of the tree.

Photosynthesis—the process by which plants use sunlight to transform water and carbon dioxide into oxygen and sugars.

Pinnate—having leaflets growing from different points along a leaf stalk (as opposed to palmate, where the leaflets originate from a single point).

Pioneer species—a fast-growing, shade-intolerant species that colonizes a site after a major disturbance.

Pitch—viscous resin produced by trees.

Pollen cone—the male reproductive structure on a conifer tree that produces pollen to fertilize the seed cones. Pollen cones are usually much smaller than seed cones.

Samara—a dry, winged fruit.

Sap—water and nutrients that flow through a tree's vascular tissues (xylem and phloem).

Sapwood—the lighter, outer portion of a tree stem's xylem. This is the part of the tree stem through which water and dissolved nutrients are transported from the roots to the crown.

Seed cone—the female reproductive structure on a conifer tree that produces seeds.

Serotinous—remaining closed for an extended period.

Serrated—having a toothed edge like a saw blade.

Shade tolerance—a trait that allows a plant to survive in low-light conditions.

Silviculture—the art and science of growing and tending forest trees.

Silvical characteristics—a tree's growth traits and tolerances.

Snag—a standing dead tree.

Softwood—a term that refers to conifer trees which, in general, have lighter density wood than broad-leaved trees.

Stand—a contiguous area of similar tree composition.

Stand dynamics—how forest stands grow and change over time and respond to disturbances.

Stipule—a structure that grows at the base of a leaf stem.

Strobile—a cone-like seed-bearing structure with overlapping scales.

Stomata—breathing pores on leaves and some stems where gases such as oxygen, carbon dioxide, and water vapor are exchanged (stomata is the plural form of stomate).

Stomatal band—a waxy stripe on a tree needle where the stomata are located.

Subalpine—relating to high elevation areas just below timberline.

Succession—the change in tree species assemblages over time, in the absence of disturbance, from fast-growing, shade-intolerant species to slower-growing, shade-tolerant species.

Symbiosis—a mutually beneficial relationship between two organisms.

Taproot—a central root that grows downward with lateral roots branching off of it.

Timberline—the highest elevation at which trees can grow.

Transpiration—the process by which water flows through a plant's vascular system and is then released to the atmosphere as water vapor.

Understory—the lower vegetation level in a forest, e.g., shrubs and herbaceous vegetation.

Vascular system—the network of conduits that carry water and dissolved nutrients within a tree or other vascular plant.

Water column—the connected stream of water from the roots to the crown of a tree, held together by the cohesive properties (i.e., the tendency to stick to one another) of water molecules.

Whorl—a group of lateral branches circling the same point on the stem of a tree. A vigorously-growing tree will typically put out a new whorl each year as it grows in height.

Windthrow—trees that are uprooted or broken by wind.

Xylem—the woody part of a tree stem, which may be composed of heartwood and sapwood.

References and Credits

Species distribution maps were derived from: U.S. Geological Survey. 1999. *Digital representation of "Atlas of United States Trees,"* by Elbert L. Little Jr. The maps were generated by Mary Ann Rozance, WSU Extension Forestry.

The following references were consulted in the development of this book and are highly recommended for further reading:

Arno, S.F. and R.P. Hammerly. 2007. *Northwest Trees.* The Mountaineers Books.

British Columbia Ministry of Forests, Lands and Natural Resources Operations. 2008. Tree species compendium. www.for.gov.bc.ca/hfp/silviculture/Compendium/index.htm.

Burns, R.M. and B.H. Honkala. 1990. *Silvics of North America.* Agriculture Handbook 654. USDA Forest Service.

Gunther, E. 1945. *Ethnobotany of western Washington: The knowledge and use of indigenous plants by Native Americans.* University of Washington Press.

Guard, J.B. 1995. *Wetland plants of Oregon and Washington.* Lone Pine Publishing.

Jacobson, A.L. and P.F. Zika. 2007 A new hybrid cherry, *Prunus xpugetensis* (P. avium x P. emarginata, Rosaceae) from the Pacific Northwest. *Madrono* 54: 74-85.

Jensen, E.C. and C.R. Ross. 2005. *Trees to know in Oregon.* EC 1450. Oregon State University Extension.

Kuhnlein, H.V. and N.J. Turner. 1991. *Traditional plant foods of Canadian indigenous peoples: Nutrition, botany, and use.* Gordon and Breach.

Mosher, M.M. and K. Lunnum. 1997. *Trees of Washington.* Washington State University Extension Bulletin EB0440.

Oliver, C.D. and B.C. Larson. 1996. *Forest stand dynamics.* John Wiley & Sons, Inc.

Pojar, J. and A. MacKinnon. 1994. *Plants of the Pacific Northwest Coast.* Lone Pine Publishing.

Seiler, J. 2010. The meanings of Latin names available at dendro.cnre.vt.edu/dendrology/syllabus/meanings.cfm.

USDA PLANTS Database. plants.usda.gov.

Index of Common and Scientific Names

spruce
    Engelmann, 108-110, 125, 126
    Sitka, 28-31, 99, 109, 125, 126
subalpine fir, 101-103, 109, 112, 125, 126
Taxus brevifolia, 39-41, 73, 85, 125, 126
Thuja plicata, 20-23, 27, 30, 105, 106, 120, 125, 126, 127
trembling aspen. *See* quaking aspen
Tsuga
    heterophylla, 16-19, 22, 25, 27, 30, 40, 91, 92, 125, 126
    mertensiana, 90-92, 96, 97, 99, 101, 125, 126
vine maple, 2, 53
western flowering dogwood. *See* Pacific dogwood
western hemlock, 16-19, 22, 25, 27, 30, 40, 91, 92, 125, 126
western redcedar, 20-23, 27, 30, 105, 106, 120, 125, 126, 127
western white pine, 32-35, 111, 112, 125, 126, 127
western yew. *See* Pacific yew
white alder, 48
white fir, 25
whitebark pine, 111-112, 125, 126
wild cherry. *See* bitter cherry or mazzard cherry
willow
    Pacific, 62-63, 64, 125, 126
    Scouler's, 62, 64-66, 125, 126
    Sitka, 66
Xanthocyparis nootkatensis. See *Callitropsis nootkatensis*
yellow cedar. *See* Alaska yellow cedar
yew, Pacific (western), 39-41, 73, 85, 125, 126

About the Author

Western Washington native Kevin W. Zobrist grew up in Redmond, where he developed a love for the woods and the outdoors. At the University of Washington, he earned bachelor's and master's degrees in forestry, and went on to become a forestry research scientist at the University of Washington. In 2007 he accepted a faculty position at Washington State University, where he serves as a regional extension forestry specialist for the north Puget Sound counties. Kevin's interests are ecology, native trees, adult education, and national parks. He lives in Everett with his wife Lisa.

Notes